ABSTRACT

This thesis will scrutinize the histories of our nation's three most prolific domestic lone wolf terrorists: Tim McVeigh, Ted Kaczynski, and Eric Rudolph. It will establish a chronological pattern to their radicalization and reveal that their communal ideological beliefs, psychology, attributes, traits, and training take place along a common chronological timeline. Their pattern of radicalization can be used as an indicator of lone wolf terrorist radicalization development in future cases. This thesis establishes a strikingly similar chronological pattern of radicalization that was present in each terrorist's biography. This pattern can identify future lone wolf terrorist radicalization activity upstream. It can provide a valuable portent to apply in the analysis of potential lone terrorists, potentially enabling law enforcement to prevent tragedies emerging from the identified population through psychological assistance, evaluation, training, or, in the worst case, detention.

THIS PAGE INTENTIONALLY LEFT BLANK

TABLE OF CONTENTS

THIS PAGE INTENTIONALLY LEFT BLANK

LIST OF ACRONYMS AND ABBREVIATIONS

AR–15	Armalite 15
ARCOM	Army Commendation Medal
ATF	Bureau of Alcohol, Tobacco, and Firearms
CBS	Columbia Broadcasting System
FBI	Federal Bureau of Investigation
FC	Freedom Club
FP	Future Proletariat
IQ	Intelligence Quotient
M–16	Rifle, Caliber 5.56 mm
MRE	Meal Ready to Eat
STRATFOR	Strategic Force
UN	United Nations

THIS PAGE INTENTIONALLY LEFT BLANK

ACKNOWLEDGMENTS

I would like to thank my thesis advisor, Professor Maria Rasmussen, for her guidance during this research project. I would also like to thank my fantastic editor, Andrea Courtright, who spent countless hours reviewing the grammatical composition of this work. Finally, my wife Rachael provided the necessary motivation for me to get this project done, both in a timely fashion and professionally. Thank you all for your contributions.

THIS PAGE INTENTIONALLY LEFT BLANK

I. PATTERNS OF RADICALIZATION: INTRODUCTION

A. MAJOR RESEARCH QUESTION

This work will focus on identifying common markers and radicalization patterns among domestic lone wolf terrorists in the United States. It will probe the histories of the three most notorious American lone wolf terrorists to determine the following: can we unearth a chronological pattern of radicalization, drawing from their commonly held ideological beliefs, psychological factors, attributes, training and education to provide law enforcement a set of criteria for identifying the emerging lone wolves in our midst? The three case studies detailed in this thesis include: Tim McVeigh—responsible for the bombing of the Alfred P. Murrah Federal Building in Oklahoma City in 1995; Eric Rudolph—responsible for the 1996 Olympic Park bombing in Atlanta, the bombings of two abortion clinics, and a lesbian bar in Alabama in 1997 and 1998; and Ted Kaczynski—nicknamed the Unabomber—responsible for mail bombings of airlines and universities between 1978 and 1996.

B. IMPORTANCE

The United States of America's terrorism focus has largely been an international one since the devastating events of September 11, 2001, pushing domestic terrorism issues to the background of the national consciousness and federal agency priority lists. Domestic terrorism poses a palpable threat, especially in times like these when so many of our best minds and resources are fixed upon foreign operations and their local terror cells. Our country has a history of homegrown domestic terrorism that should not be ignored.

By pinpointing a common set of ideological beliefs, psychological patterns, attributes, traits, training, and educational data focused on lone wolf patterns of radicalization, we could potentially intervene upstream while they were still developing as criminals, and before they carried out their large-scale attacks. We could better secure our campuses, places of worship, neighborhoods, and everything we hold dear. On the other hand, we could place one more piece in the challenging puzzle that is domestic lone wolf terrorism prevention. A great deal of existing literature is written about domestic lone wolf terrorism (discussed below); however, little is published comparing the three terrorists who are the focus of this thesis. In addition, no literature exists that attempts to synchronize and cross-reference the strikingly similar patterns of radicalization with the purpose of formulating warning signs, markers, or identifying patterns of domestic lone wolf terrorism.

C.   PROBLEMS AND HYPOTHESES

A great deal of mental capital and analysis has been focused on lone wolf terrorism for the past decade. While we learned a great deal about how individuals become radicalized in groups, much less has been ascertained about how individual lone wolves become radicalized. This thesis will scrutinize that aspect of lone wolf terrorism. If the communal ideological beliefs, psychology, attributes, traits, training, and education of the three lone wolf terrorists in this study can be ascertained and shown to take place along a common chronological timeline, then a pattern can be formulated to define radicalization, that can be used as an indicator of the development of future lone wolf terrorist radicalization. Could creating such a chronological pattern to domestic lone wolf radicalization decrease the likelihood of future attacks, by providing a valuable portent and series of markers that could then be applied in the analysis of potential lone terrorists, enabling law enforcement to prevent tragedies emerging from the identified population through psychological assistance, evaluation, training, or, in the worst case, detention?

Striking similarities existed between McVeigh, Kaczynski, and Rudolph, and a distinctive, specific pattern of radicalization was at the forefront of those similarities. Their radicalization patterns developed along stunningly similar chronological timelines. Their childhood and adolescent years conditioned them to develop similarly impaired social skills that both isolated them from society, and hobbled their ability to establish intimate human relationships or attract female companionship.

They all had a desire to belong to a group, but failed repeatedly. A lifetime of isolation and loneliness shaped them into survivalists. After attempting to fit in, find a group, and be accepted, each man turned to the one thing that could not reject him—his ideology. A turning point existed in each of their lives, at which point their ideologies demanded they submit themselves wholeheartedly to their own doctrines. This turning point is where the real radicalization began, the point where their ideology could no longer be explained through dialogue or debate, but instead through action.

Once each man submitted himself to his ideology, he would slowly stew in isolation, honing and perfecting his rigid dogma over a number of years, until he would finally strike. Once the attacks began, each man valued his individual safety, and did not place himself in harm's way. Each believed he was vital to his ideology's exposure to and acceptance by society. During their attacks, they yearned to be heard, understood, and possibly even applauded by the American public. Even though each had never found success in a group, they associated themselves and their terrorist actions with groups they made up in hopes of attracting Americans to join the cause. If they could not blend into a group, at the very least they should be able to successfully lead their own groups, governed by the very doctrines that drove them to action in the first place. Even after each of their captures, they never denounced their rigid ideologies, and were drastically concerned with how they would be remembered, and what legacies they would leave for future generations.

D.   METHOD

This thesis uses the comparative method utilizing three qualitative case studies. This method facilitates a structured, focused comparison across the cases that will produce results. Each of the three domestic lone wolf terrorists will represent a case. The structure of each case study is the same to both standardize the analysis of each terrorist and logically sequence the information. Each case study will chronologically describe each terrorist's childhood and upbringing, education, psychological factors, ideology, turning point where ideology dictated action, terrorist campaign, capture, aftermath, and finally synthesize those factors to provide an analysis of each terrorist.

Once each individual analysis is completed examining their commonly held ideological beliefs, psychological factors, attributes, and training, the final chapter will demonstrate the specific identical chronologies that existed between these three men as they radicalized to become lone wolf terrorists.

E.   LITERATURE REVIEW

Literature and research in the field of terrorism prevention and study has rapidly multiplied since September 11, 2001. It is understandable the focus has been upon international terrorist threats when one considers the origin of 9/11. While much has been done to advance the world's understanding of international terrorism, domestic terrorism prevention has received far less effort. Terrorism is best defined as "the use or threat of use of violence to achieve political objectives, when such violence is intended to control a population through fear or coerce a government into granting certain concessions."[1] I have found this to be the most standard, straightforward definition available and very similar to competing definitions in the academic community. Domestic terrorism is defined by the Federal Bureau of Investigation as:

> the unlawful use, or threatened use, of violence by a group or individuals based and operating entirely within the United States (or its territories) without foreign direction, committed against persons or property to intimidate or coerce a government, the civilian population, or any segment thereof, in furtherance of political or social objectives.[2]

Lone Wolf Terrorism is best defined by STRATFOR, the largest Web publisher of geopolitical intelligence in the world, as "a person who acts on his or her own without orders from—or even connections to—an organization."[3] Terry Turchie (a 20-year veteran FBI agent who led the FBI's effort to capture both Kaczynski and Rudolph), and Kathleen Puckett (a 23-year veteran of the FBI and clinical psychologist who served as the lead profiler for both the Kaczynski and Rudolph hunts), have completed a vast

---

[1] Maria Jose Moyano, *Argentina's Lost Patrol* (New Haven, CT: Yale University Press, 1995), 3.

[2] Federal Bureau of Investigation, "Congressional Testimony 2002: "The threat of Eco-Terrorism," Federal Bureau of Investigation, http://www.fbi.gov/congress/congress02/jarboe021202.htm.

[3] Fred Burton and Scott Stewart, "The Lone Wolf Disconnect," STRATFOR Global Intelligence, January 30, 2008, http://www.stratfor.com/weekly/lone_wolf_disconnect.

amount of research on lone wolf terrorism in the United States. Their book *Hunting the American Terrorist: The FBI's War on Homegrown Terror*[4] is an analysis of the lessons learned by the FBI as they hunted lone terrorists in the United States between 1993 and 2001.

The authors use the FBI manhunts of lone wolf terrorists Theodore Kaczynski and Eric Rudolph and the case files of eight other lone terrorists to create a profile of the lone wolf terrorist in the United States. In order to establish the most representative conglomerate of lone wolfs, Kathleen Pucket uses six criteria that best characterize the lone wolves in our midst. The following criteria are useful in defining what conditions constitute lone terrorist activity in the United States:

1. The terrorist act was conceived and executed by one or a few individuals not operating in the context of an organized group.

2. There was conscious acceptance of lethal violence as a means to achieving an ideological, political, or religious goal.

3. Although personal motivations for lethal violence might be present, accomplishing a larger ideological, political, or religious goal was always a primary objective.

4. There was conscious acceptance of the possibility of death or injury to third parties not associated with the primary target.

5. It did not appear that the perpetrator(s) intended suicide.

6. Homicide resulted from the act, or would have resulted had law enforcement or other circumstances not intervened.[5]

The analysis of lone terrorists provided by this book was extremely useful. It identified many characteristics and traits that were similar to lone terrorists, including the three studied in this thesis; however, it failed to establish the chronological pattern of radicalization so central to this thesis. Nevertheless, it was determined through the course of this research that many similarities existed between these findings and that of Turchie and Puckett's larger study of lone terrorism.

---

[4] Terry Turchie and Kathleen Puckett, *Hunting the American Terrorist: The FBI's War on Homegrown Terror* (Palisades, NY: History Publishing Company, 2007).

[5] Ibid., 240–241.

Bruce Hoffman warns of the dangers inherent in a domestic lone wolf terrorist strike. Hoffman stated, "Besides the 1993 World Trade Center bombing and the attack of September 11, 2001, the nation's most significant terrorist plots and attacks were by men acting alone or in pairs without ties to known radical networks."[6] Hoffman goes on to identify the most effective lone wolf terrorists in our history:

> [Their] ranks include Theodore Kaczynski, Timothy McVeigh and Eric Rudolph.....I think this is one of the major challenges that we face in the U.S. The major incidents in the U.S. have not conformed to our stereotype of an established terror organization attacking a major iconic landmark.[7]

Hoffman's warning is stern. Domestic terrorism in the United States today may be more of a threat than international terrorism. The domestic terrorist threat in our country, and specifically the study of lone wolf terrorism, require further study.

The literature on Timothy McVeigh is vast. His story is most thoroughly documented because McVeigh carried out the most successful and deadliest domestic terrorist event in our nation's history, with the bombing of the Alfred P. Murrah Federal Building in Oklahoma City, Oklahoma on April 19, 1995. The primary sources used to research Timothy McVeigh include three books, the FBI Web site, the Oklahoma City FBI field office, and a number of magazine and journal articles.

American Terrorist[8], written by reporters Lou Michel and Dan Herbeck, who grew up near McVeigh's hometown of Buffalo, New York, is the best known of the three major studies on Tim McVeigh. The book will be valuable to this research, because it focuses on the chronological sequences of Tim McVeigh's life beginning with his childhood, and culminating with his interviews while in prison following the bombing. Also critical to the understanding of McVeigh, is Brandon Stickney's book, *All American*

---

[6] Associated Press, "Potential 'lone wolf' attackers concern police: Officials worry about disaffected men forming terrorism's next violent wave," MSNBC, http://www.msnbc.msn.com/id/8888865.

[7] Ibid.

[8] Lou Michel and Dan Herbeck, *American Terrorist* (New York: HarperCollins Publishers, 2001).

Monster: The Unauthorized Biography of Timothy McVeigh.[9] Stickney, a local news reporter from the *Union Sun & Journal* in Lockport, New York, worked directly with McVeigh to write the book. McVeigh considered this book his biography. It offers a chronological view of Tim McVeigh's life, but focuses more on answering the question of why he committed the act. The author analyzes the psychological aspects of Tim McVeigh, his writings, and his commitment to his ideology.

Finally, *Secrets Worth Dying For*[10] is written by David Hammer and Jeff Paul, two inmates on death row who served time with Tim McVeigh at the United States Penitentiary in Terre Haute, Indiana. This book is the best source available to help one understand Timothy McVeigh's beliefs, commitment, character, and reflections on his crimes. There seems no better way to glimpse the soul of a man like McVeigh than from the firsthand accounts of the inmates who McVeigh befriended, trusted, and with whom he spent his final days.

Numerous journals, magazines, and news reports detail both the life of Tim McVeigh and the bombing. This thesis will highlight the best of these sources, while listing the others that will be used in the bibliography section. "The Matter of Tim McVeigh," a *TIME* magazine article from 1995, details McVeigh's educational background and provides an excellent interview from the period of his trial. "An Ordinary Boy's Extraordinary Rage; After a Long Search for Order, Timothy McVeigh Finally Found a World He Could Fit," is a *Washington Post* article by Dale Russakoff and Serge Kovaleski from 1995 that attempts to demonstrate that "the roots of McVeigh's extremism are clearly traceable to his youth."[11] Finally, "Behind the Lone Terrorist, a Pack Mentality," was written by Mike German, and details lone wolf terrorism in the United States. The article describes Timothy McVeigh's actions, stating "Lone extremism is not a phenomenon; it's a technique, a ruse designed to subvert the criminal

---

[9] Brandon Stickney, *All-American Monster: The Unauthorized Biography of Timothy McVeigh* (New York: Prometheus Books, 1996).

[10] David Hammer and Jeffrey Paul, *Secrets Worth Dying For* (Bloomington, IN: 1st Books Library, 2004).

[11] Dale Russakoff and Serge Kovaleski, "An Ordinary Boy's Extraordinary Rage; After a Long Search for Order, Timothy McVeigh Finally Found a World He Could Fit Into," *The Washington Post*, July 2, 1995, A1.

justice system."[12]   This article offers a different perspective into the life, purpose, and methods of a lone wolf terrorist, using Tim McVeigh as a case study, and will help to complete the picture.

Theodore Kaczynski stands as the smartest, most educated domestic lone wolf terrorist in our nation's history. He is most famous for terrorist acts involving both universities and airlines. The FBI dubbed him the Unabomber during their investigation and subsequent pursuit of Kaczynski. Numerous books, magazine articles, and journals depict Kaczynski's life, terrorist activities, beliefs, and eventual capture.

There is no better piece of literature to help one understand the psychology of Theodore Kaczynski than the book, *The Unabomber Manifesto: Industrial Society and Its Future*[13], written by the Unabomber himself. This book outlines his goals and describes what, in his opinion, is wrong with the world. Kaczynski asserts the civilized world is failing because of technology, globalization, and competition. He warns that while many of the most industrialized nations will benefit in the short term, the world will pay the price in the long term. While executing his terrorist activities and attempting to evade the massive U.S. manhunt to capture him, Kaczynski threatened to kill more people if his manifesto was not published in a respectable newspaper. He offered it to the *New York Times,* which printed the full text, and the *Washington Post,* who printed a summary. The manifesto was released as a book in 2007.

A second book was written by a fellow classmate, describing Kaczynski's education at Harvard. Alston Chase wrote *A Mind for Murder: The Education of the Unabomber and the Origins of Modern Terrorism*[14] in 2007.   This book is a chronological study of the life of Kaczynski and brings to the forefront new details of Kaczynski's troubled childhood. It also thoroughly covers Kaczynski's academic career from grade school through his doctoral program in mathematics and his teaching career at

---

[12] Mike German, "Behind the Lone Terrorist, a Pack Mentality," *The Washington Post*, June 5, 2005, B1.

[13] Theodore Kaczynski, *The Unabomber Manifesto: Industrial Society & Its Future* (Minneapolis, MN: Filiquarian Publishing, LLC, 1998).

[14] Alston Chase, *A Mind for Murder: The Education of the Unabomber and the Origins of Modern Terrorism* (New York: W.W. Norton & Co., 2004).

U.C. Berkeley. Finally, the book discusses his retreat from academia to the isolated forests of Montana and chronologically describes each terrorist attack he conducted.

The final book written on Kaczynski explores the twenty-five years he lived in the forests of Montana. The book *Unabomber: The Secret Life of Ted Kaczynski* [15] meticulously details Kaczynski's years alone in the forest and hypothesizes why Kaczynski committed acts of terror. One of the books author's, Chris Waits, was Kaczynski's neighbor for the twenty-five years he lived in the forest. The book attempts to explain Kaczynski's reasoning through both excerpts from his journal, recovered from his cabin after his arrest, and from face-to-face discussions with Chris Waits. There are few people, if any, who knew Theodore Kaczynski as well as his friend Chris Waits, especially in the years immediately preceding his capture.

A couple of newspaper and magazine articles are worthy of mention at this point. The *Washington Post's* Serge Kovaleski wrote an excellent article on the Kaczynski family, which provides a revealing perspective on Kaczynski's childhood. The article "His Brother's Keeper"[16] tells the story of David Kaczynski, the Unabomber's brother, describes the brothers growing up together, and David's realization that his brother was the man the FBI wanted. David Kaczynski provides excellent insight on his brother's childhood and his metamorphosis into a lone wolf terrorist. Additionally, David describes when his brother's behavior began to turn abnormal and what he tried to do to help him.

Finally, *USA Today's* Richard Vatz and Lee Weinberg produced an excellent article depicting Kaczynski's trial. The article "The Unabomber's Twisted Saga"[17] details Kaczynski's trial as well as personal conferences and discussions with his defense counsel. The world expected Kaczynski's defense to include an insanity plea; however,

---

[15] Chris Waits and David Shors, *Unabomber: The Secret Life of Ted* Kaczynski (Helena, MT: Helena Independent Record and Montana Magazine,1999).

[16] Serge Kovaleski, "His Brother's Keeper," *The Washington Post*, July 10, 2001, B6.

[17] Richard Vatz and Lee Weinberg, "The Unabomber's twisted saga," *USA Today*, July 1998, 5.

Kaczynski maintained to his defense counsel that he was perfectly sane and refused any tests that could prove the opposite. It would be difficult to find a more detailed, comprehensive article depicting Kaczynski's trial.

Eric Rudolph is considered one of the most prolific domestic lone wolf terrorists in U.S. history. Rudolph is most famous for bombing Centennial Olympic Park on July 27, 1996 during the Olympic Games in Atlanta. Additionally, Rudolph is responsible for bombing abortion clinics in both Sandy Springs, Alabama, on January 16, 1997 and Birmingham, Alabama, on January 29, 1998. He is also responsible for the bombing of an Atlanta lesbian bar on February 21, 1997. Ample literature depicting his life, beliefs, terrorist activity, and capture exists in the form of books, scholarly journals and magazine articles. This literature coupled with available FBI data will serve as the primary sources for this case study.

Maryanne Vollers has contributed more to the understanding of Eric Rudolph than any other scholar. Her research into Rudolph's life is represented in her two books. Her most recent book, *Lone Wolf: Eric Rudolph and the Legacy of American Terror*[18], focuses on Eric Rudolph the man. It examines his life, beliefs, and reasons for becoming a terrorist. The book effectively humanizes Rudolph while chronicling the events of his life and the radicalization of his beliefs. Although the book thoroughly details his terrorist life, its insight into his journey past the threshold of violence is central to understanding Eric Rudolph. Vollers' other book, *Lone Wolf: Eric Rudolph: Murder, Myth, and the Pursuit of an American Outlaw,*[19] expertly describes Rudolph's terrorist activities and details how he executed them. This book depicts Rudolph's complex, well-planned and executed attacks, illuminating the image of an intelligent, patient, calculating man committed to his cause and beliefs rather than reinforcing the image of the homicidal maniac the U.S. media espoused.

---

[18] Maryanne Vollers, *Lone Wolf: Eric Rudolph and the Legacy of American Terror* (New York: Harper Perennial Publishing Company, 2007).

[19] Maryanne Vollers, *Lone Wolf: Eric Rudolph: Murder, Myth, and the Pursuit of an American Outlaw* (New York: HarperCollins, 2006).

Henry Schuster and Charles Stone contributed a detailed account of the FBI hunt for Eric Rudolph in their book *Hunting Eric Rudolph: An Insider's Account of the Five-Year Search for the Olympic Bomber.*[20] The book chronologically details Rudolph's life and depicts his final years evading authorities in detail. Kathleen Walls also studies Rudolph's life in her book *Man Hunt: The Eric Rudolph Story.*[21] Kathleen Walls scrutinizes Rudolph's childhood and upbringing, as well as his association with Christian extremist organizations, and his pattern of radicalization.

A number of respected newspapers, magazine, and professional journal articles cover both the FBI's manhunt of Rudolph in 2005, and his trial. A professional journal article published by the *Law Enforcement News,*[22] described Rudolph's demeanor as he addressed victims of his Olympic Park bombing at his trial. Rudolph was forced to first make a public apology to his victims, and then listen as each one described his or her injuries. This article explores Rudolph's mental state at the time of his trial.

The *Christian Science Monitor* published an excellent article on Rudolph in 2003 entitled "How did Eric Rudolph Survive?"[23] This article details how Rudolph evaded the FBI for over five years in the mountains of North Carolina. The article examines exactly how Rudolph managed to survive and garner the support of the locals during this time. Additionally, the article discusses Rudolph's religious affiliations and the ideology that fueled his terrorist activities. *TIME* magazine's Paul Cuadros and company, produced an excellent article on the capture of Eric Rudolph in 2003. The article, "How Luck Ran Out for a Most Wanted Fugitive,"[24] depicts the complexity of the FBI's manhunt to capture Eric Rudolph. This article details Rudolph's final days as a fugitive evading authorities, and the break that led the FBI to finally apprehend him.

---

[20] Henry Schuster and Charles Stone, *Hunting Eric Rudolph: An Insider's Account of the Five-Year Search for the Olympic Bomber* (New York: Berkley Publishing Group, 2005).

[21] Kathleen Walls, *Man Hunt: The Eric Rudolph Story* (LaVergne, TN: Global Authors Publications, 2003).

[22] Nancy Egan, "Hunting Eric Rudolph," *Law Enforcement News* (2005): Vol 31, Issue 636, S5–S7.

[23] Patrik Jonsson, "How did Eric Rudolph Survive?" *The Christian Science Monitor*, June 4, 2003, 4.

[24] Paul Cuadros et al., "How luck ran out for a most wanted fugitive," *TIME*, June 9, 2003, 8.

Ample research and analysis is available on Tim McVeigh, Ted Kaczynski, and Eric Rudolph. Each of their individual life stories is copiously detailed. Expert studies and analysis on lone wolf terrorists, like those presented by former FBI agents Terry Turchie and Kathleen Puckett, are abundant, and provide the critical context necessary to a successful study like this. Through research, it was discovered that a fissure exists between the individual analysis of McVeigh, Kaczynski, and Rudolph's life stories, and the expert analysis on lone wolf terrorists. The individual accounts available simply provide the raw facts and story of each terrorist. The larger studies on lone terrorism provide common traits, beliefs, and analogous trends of lone terrorists, but they lack chronology. This thesis fills the fissure by analyzing each individual terrorist's story, using the larger lone terror studies for context and direction, and then applying and comparing them to each other to construct a communal chronological pattern of radicalization. This chronological pattern of radicalization can be used as an indicator, or at least another light along the winding maze of future lone wolf terrorist radicalization.

F.   THESIS OVERVIEW

This thesis consists of five major sections. Chapter I contains an introduction, research question, an explanation of this study's relevance, problems and hypothesis, research method, literature review, and road map. Chapters II, III, and IV focus on Timothy McVeigh, Ted Kaczynski, and Eric Rudolph's patterns of radicalization, respectively. Chapter V will synthesize the information and detail the chronological pattern of radicalization that these three terrorists share, building a specific, common vignette of a lone wolf terrorist pattern of radicalization, which will aid law enforcement in profiling and researching communities in a better understanding of the complex problem.

II.   TIM MCVEIGH: PATTERNS OF RADICALIZATION

Timothy McVeigh carried out the most successful and deadliest domestic terrorist event in our nation's history, with the bombing of the Alfred P. Murrah Federal Building in Oklahoma City, Oklahoma on April 19, 1995. The Federal Bureau of Investigation states that McVeigh "was the prototypical lone wolf terrorist"[25] in the United States. This chapter will examine Timothy McVeigh's life in an effort to determine which events changed McVeigh from an intelligent, middle class, decorated Army veteran to a radical, lone wolf, domestic terrorist responsible for the death of 168 American citizens and the wounding of over 500. The study of McVeigh's pattern of radicalization and his associated ideological beliefs, psychology, attributes, traits, training, and education is important to both our understanding of why he executed this deadly attack, and how we as a country can prevent future attacks.

A.   CHILDHOOD AND UPBRINGING

Timothy McVeigh was born on April 23, 1968, to a middle-class catholic family. He grew up in the predominantly white towns of Lockport and Pendleton, New York. Bill McVeigh, Timothy's father, was a quiet, traditional man whose commitment to the long hours of work that provided extra income and a higher standard of living for his family, reflected his conviction that his role as provider was paramount. Mickey McVeigh, Timothy's mother, hailed from a very traditional family in which gender roles were honored and observed. A woman's place was in the home, caring for her family. Although Mickey did not fully buy into this limited definition of womanhood, she soon pleased her mother by giving birth shortly after she married and electing to stay home with her baby daughter, Patricia. Timothy was born next, followed by his sister Jennifer. Mickey's   role   as   a   stay-at-home   mom   would   not   last   long;   she   became

---

[25] Mike German, "Behind the Lone Terrorist, a Pack Mentality," *The Washington Post,* June 5, 2005, A3.

a stewardess when Tim was five, and traveled often. With both parents immersed in their jobs, McVeigh often joked that he "was one of the original latch-key kids, long before the term became popular."[26]

The story of McVeigh's childhood fits the description of nearly every boy's in the United States. He was a rambunctious, mischievous little boy with an active imagination, who early on, was very happy. McVeigh cared greatly for animals and had a lot of compassion and empathy for them. One day, McVeigh saw a neighbor boy throw a sack into the pond near his house. McVeigh later investigated and was dismayed to discover the boy's sack was filled with kittens.

> For McVeigh who loved animals, and especially kittens, the realization of what he had witnessed hit him hard. He cried about the incident for days.[27]

Weeks later McVeigh's cat attacked and killed a helpless rabbit while he watched. He could do nothing to save the rabbit. He felt horrible. Reflecting on these two events, McVeigh cited "both incidents as landmarks in his growing awareness that life is about difficult decisions."[28]

Bullies began to target McVeigh when he turned ten years old. He was scrawny, uncoordinated, and small for his size, which made him an easy mark. McVeigh dealt with the escalating problem in the only way he knew how, by secluding himself from others.

> [He] became more of a loner, where he would escape into a world of fantasy and make believe. Like heroes from his comic books, he would create scenarios of revenge to atone for past moments of weakness and to defeat his enemies.[29]

---

[26] David Hammer and Jeffrey Paul, *Secrets Worth Dying For* (Bloomington, IN: 1st Books Library, 2004), 15.

[27] Lou Michel and Dan Herbeck, *American Terrorist* (New York: HarperCollins Publishers, 2001), 19.

[28] Ibid., 20.

[29] Hammer and Paul, *Secrets Worth Dying For,* 14.

McVeigh hated injustice, and even as a young boy, had a strong belief that the world was a struggle of good vs. evil.

McVeigh's parents were divorced in 1979, just before he turned eleven. Although they would make a few attempts to reconcile, the marriage would ultimately fail. McVeigh immediately sided with his father and blamed his mother for their troubles. The separation "did scar McVeigh and set into motion feelings of anger and hatred toward women who 'don't know their place is to be at home, raising children and supporting their husbands.'"[30] McVeigh's mother broke up the family and took McVeigh's two sisters to Florida for a few months. McVeigh and his father stayed put and made the best of the situation. McVeigh's mother returned with the girls months later, to reunite the family, because she felt the children needed to live together. This would only last for a short period of time. For McVeigh, the damage had been done; he was not especially interested in his mother or his sisters for many years to come.

For McVeigh, living with his father after the divorce further contributed to his path toward isolation. His father worked long hours and rarely addressed his son's needs much beyond his basic necessities. From age eleven on, Tim would gain an independence that not many boys his age possessed. He spent long hours by himself, forced into isolation and caring for himself at a very early age. Nurture was largely absent from his life. Research on the subject of nature vs. nurture by psychologist David Reece in his book *The Relationship Code,* suggests, "Many genetic factors, powerful as they may be in psychological development, exert their influence only through the good offices of the family and that means that how parents raise their children actually does matter."[31] Family time was non-existent in the McVeigh household. Tim's parents equated taking care of their family with providing them the basics. McVeigh's childhood was difficult; however, his adolescent years would prove even more challenging.

---

[30] Hammer and Paul, *Secrets Worth Dying For,* 14.

[31] Sharon Begley, "The Nature of Nurturing," *Newsweek*, March 27, 2000, Volume 135, 64.

B. TRAINING, EDUCATION, AND FOUNDATIONS OF IDEOLOGY

After McVeigh's parents went their separate ways, the most influential person in his life quickly became his grandfather, Ed McVeigh. The younger McVeigh spent real quality time with his grandfather and considered him his mentor. His grandfather would introduce him to what would become the greatest passion of his life: guns. Ed, an avid gun collector himself, bought McVeigh his first gun at the age of thirteen. From that moment on, the two would spend countless hours together, bonding over their guns. Ed McVeigh would teach Timothy everything he knew about guns and "under Edward's watchful eye, McVeigh seemed to bloom with the gun, an excitement unmatched in other activities he attempted."[32] From the age of thirteen on, McVeigh would make guns and the collection of guns his number one hobby and passion. "For McVeigh, the gun was nourishment for his self esteem."[33] Guns seemed to be the great equalizer in his life, the more proficient he made himself with guns, the more confident he felt.

McVeigh began to show psychological signs of paranoia and delusion at the age of fourteen, when he delved deeper into his fantasy world, imagining himself in constant peril. After immersing himself in his comic books depicting the struggle of good vs. evil, and watching movies like *The Omega Man," "Logan's Run," "Red Dawn," "The Planet of the Apes,"[34]* and *"The Last Day,"[35]* all depicting the coming of World War III or the impending struggle for humanity, McVeigh became obsessed with the notion that he must be ready to defend himself, his family, and his country. At 14, McVeigh confided that he was a survivalist, stockpiling food, camping equipment, and weapons "in

---

[32] Brandon Stickney, *All-American Monster: The Unauthorized Biography of Timothy McVeigh* (New York: Prometheus Books, 1996) 65.

[33] Michel and Herbeck, *American Terrorist,* 27.

[34] Ibid., 47.

[35] Stickney, *All American Monster,* 72.

case of a nuclear attack or the communists took over the country."[36] This ideology played right into McVeigh's love for guns and he was convinced he could not have too many when the desperate hour came.

Academics were not very important to McVeigh, although he was one of the brightest students in his school. "McVeigh was a bright (IQ 128, above average), hardworking student who got sloppy at times but earned mostly As and Bs through high school, falling just outside the top 20% of his class."[37] McVeigh's intelligence surprised his teachers when his senior year he "earned a five-hundred-dollar Regents scholarship for college because he scored well on his tests."[38] McVeigh would go to junior college and study business for a couple months but soon he dropped out of school. He returned to dead end jobs and felt something significant was missing from his life. He was more concerned with the now, with making money so he could buy a car, more guns, and survival gear. During high school, McVeigh would hold jobs at both Burger King and a camping supply store to make his money. He began to focus all his energy reading survival magazines, government conspiracy books and articles, and holding target practice with his guns.

McVeigh found the perfect job working for a security company as a security guard protecting armored cars. This was a great match for McVeigh because it allowed him to both obtain a license to carry a gun and feel as if he were part of something big. He started out shakily, and was almost fired his very first week of work. After obtaining his weapons permit, McVeigh showed up at work one day with a bandoleer of shotgun shells strewn across his chest. McVeigh's supervisor thought it was a bit alarming, but played off the whole incident, blaming McVeigh's overzealousness on his youth. The supervisor sent McVeigh home to change into appropriate clothing. The security company job also broadened McVeigh's horizons a bit because some of his cash pick-up sites were located in impoverished areas of Buffalo, New York. It was on these days that

---

[36] Dale Russakoff and Serge Kovaleski, "An Ordinary Boy's Extraordinary Rage; After a Long Search for Order, Timothy McVeigh Finally Found a World He Could Fit Into," *The Washington Post*, July 2, 1995, A1.

[37] George Church, "The Matter of Tim McVeigh," *Time,* August 14, 1995, 40.

[38] Stickney, *All American Monster, 78.*

McVeigh would come into contact with under privileged populations. It angered him to see the free handouts people received in the unemployment lines. McVeigh's co-workers did not mask their racist ideologies when work took them into poor areas. McVeigh, who grew up in an all-white area, quickly picked up the racist ideas possessed by his co-workers. They would often say, "there they are—the porch monkeys… they sit on their porch all month waiting for the welfare checks to come in."[39] McVeigh willingly participated in the racist banter. He truly abhorred the fact that while he was working his tail off every day on the armored car, these people were getting free money for doing nothing. McVeigh despised that the government would have such a policy to so blindly hand out money to people who obviously did not deserve it.

McVeigh realized that his security guard job was not going to take him very far. It had given him a decent, steady paycheck, which enabled him to further his readiness within the survivalist culture. McVeigh purchased an AR-15, a semi-automatic rifle modeled after the Army's M-16, and around the same time, bought ten acres of land in Buffalo. "McVeigh told friends that the land was to be a survivalist bunker."[40] McVeigh would spend days alone or with friends on his land both shooting his guns, and experimenting with homemade explosives. McVeigh was proud that he had earned enough money to buy his own land. It made him feel as if he were starting to make it in the world; however, he could not get over the fact that the security job was the best he could find. It did not make sense to him that a man of his talents could not find work that paid good money. After many weeks of complaining to his father, it was his father who finally encouraged McVeigh to join the Army. Many McVeigh men had served in the Army and found the training and lifestyle served them well, too. Bill McVeigh figured it would be a perfect match for his son who loved weapons, adventure, and the outdoors. The Army provided a structured framework within which McVeigh could enjoy all of those things.

---

[39] Michel and Herbeck, *American Terrorist,* 51.

[40] Russakoff and Kovaleski, "An Ordinary Boy's Extraordinary Rage," A2.

C.   LIFE IN THE MILITARY

On May 24, 1988, McVeigh joined the United States Army. During basic training at Fort Benning, Georgia, McVeigh "would meet two buddies who would become an indelible part of his life story."[41] Terry Nichols shared many of McVeigh's beliefs about 2nd Amendment rights and Michael Fortier had radical views of his own, making them suitable companions for McVeigh. McVeigh and Nichols developed a close bond and friendship at Fort Benning. After basic training, McVeigh was assigned as an Infantryman in the 1st Infantry Division at Fort Riley, Kansas. He was a good Soldier, technically and tactically. McVeigh, Nichols, and Fortier were all stationed at Fort Riley within two months of each other, and their friendship continued to grow. "McVeigh and Nichols were 'hard into guns,' in long talks, they discovered both were survivalists who believed warnings in gun magazines that the government would take away their weapons."[42]

McVeigh, a top Soldier in his Company, would become one of the Top Bradley Fighting Vehicle Gunners in his Battalion, attaining a perfect score twice on Bradley gunnery table 8. McVeigh had come out of his shell as a Soldier. He was good at it and everyone knew it. Even so, his buddies suspected that Tim had an odd, dark side. His long interest in survivalist tactics became consuming. Army friends have said that he "rented a storage shed in nearby Junction City, and just as he had done at his father's home back in Pendleton, he kept one hundred gallons of fresh water there, along with guns, ammunition, MRE rations, and other supplies."[43] He fretted over his Second Amendment rights. "He pored over survivalist magazines and was seen dog-earring 'The Turner Diaries,' a racist anti-government novel about bombing the FBI headquarters in Washington."[44] McVeigh isolated himself, frequently spending weekends alone in his barracks room. His buddies also found it strange that McVeigh was not interested in

---

[41] Michel and Herbeck, *American Terrorist,* 64.

[42] Russakoff and Kovaleski, "An Ordinary Boy's Extraordinary Rage," A4.

[43] Michel and Herbeck, *American Terrorist,* 70.

[44] Lois Romano, "An Enigma Awaits Death; Tim McVeigh Was a Good Kid and a Good Soldier. So What Went Wrong?," *The Washington Post,* May 4, 2001, A1.

pursuing a social life or young women. Even when he, by chance, found himself in the company of women, he acted nervous, awkward, and inappropriate. On one rare night out, McVeigh sidled up to a bar, and quipped to a woman he had just met:

> Okay we've just met. We could sit here for three hours wasting money on drinks, or we could just go now and get laid.[45]

It did not take many rejections for McVeigh to stop trying.

In January 1991, McVeigh was deployed with his unit to the Gulf War. SGT McVeigh performed well as a Bradley gunner and was awarded the Army Commendation Medal (ARCOM). The ARCOM stated, "He inspired other members of his platoon by destroying an enemy machine-gun emplacement, killing two Iraqi Soldiers, and forcing the surrender of thirty others from dug-in positions."[46] McVeigh's combat experience weighed heavily on his conscience. He decided the U.S. government was simply bullying Iraq. It shamed him to think he, by extension, had become something that he had despised his whole life, a bully. McVeigh became convinced the U.S. invaded Iraq as an excuse to steal that country's oil. For McVeigh, it was the perfect example of the government conspiracy that he had fantasized about and prepared for his whole life.

After the Gulf War, McVeigh got his shot at a coveted spot with Army Special Forces. He ended up washing out of Special Forces selection because he wasn't in good shape after his deployment, and was ill equipped to achieve the minimum time requirements on the foot marches. Although McVeigh was given the option to try again months later, he harbored anger over failing the first time and he elected to leave the Army. After three and a half years of service, McVeigh received an honorable discharge from the Army in December of 1991. Nichols and Fortier also left the U.S. Army during the downsizing of the force that followed the Gulf War. Although their mutual military careers came to an end, the three of them would continue their association through the bombing of the Murrah Building in 1995, their trials and prison sentences, and the eventual execution of Timothy McVeigh.

---

[45] Michel and Herbeck, *American Terrorist,* 73.

[46] Stickney, *All American Monster,* 113.

Timothy McVeigh was angry with himself for failing to make it through Special Forces selection. He did not have what it takes. His Gulf War experience left him depressed and bitter with the government for taking action against a country unable to defend itself. Still, McVeigh was proud of his Army experience as a whole. He had served very successfully in the Infantry branch. McVeigh was recognized for action in combat, and Officers had tried to talk him into re-enlisting in the Army. He felt as if his nation owed him a debt of gratitude. McVeigh anticipated the sky would be the limit when he got home, job offers would abound, and people would respect him like never before. Once home, reality smacked McVeigh in the face. Nothing had changed for him. Kudos and praise were not offered, jobs were unavailable, and the locals simply did not care about his service to the country. It was as if he had never left. McVeigh wound up taking a security job much like he had prior to enlisting in the Army. This was still the best job he could find.

McVeigh felt rage toward the system and began to isolate himself further. Richard Pearlstein describes this phenomenon in his book *The Mind of a Political Terrorist* when discussing the effects of rage and narcissistic injury. He states that when "an individual flew into a rage is to imply that he is so far overhead of reality as to have a necessarily unfocused perception of reality."[47] He goes on to say that this narcissistic rage

> ...all pertain(s) to one vital, unifying concept: the shielding or protection of the ego or self from damage, harm, guilt, or shame through 1) the veritable unleashing of heretofore repressed narcissistic rage, 2) the energizing of regulatory narcissism, and 3) accompanying regression to some manifestation of secondary narcissism. This process, which might result in an extensive range of behavior, would culminate ideally in the restoration or reinforcement of wounded self-esteem or damaged self-image.[48]

---

[47] Richard Pearlstein, *The Mind of a Political Terrorist* (Wilmington, DE: Scholarly Resources Inc., 1991), 34.

[48] Ibid.

In isolation, McVeigh, filled with rage and the unquestioning belief that he had been wronged, would fantasize over how his world should be.

Trapped in a dead end job, McVeigh became more desperate by the day. He began to write anti-government letters to the editors of local New York newspapers as his psychological release. McVeigh vented his anger on a wide range of topics like federal taxes, the erosion of second amendment rights, health care, and the decline of America. In one letter he wrote on February 11, 1992, he concluded his editorial with what would later become a famous McVeigh phrase. He stated:

> America is in serious decline. We have no proverbial tea to dump. Should we instead sink a ship full of Japanese imports? Is civil war imminent? Do we have to shed blood to reform the current system? I hope it doesn't come to that but it might.[49]

McVeigh's paranoia with the government continued to grow and he began to believe the vivid fantasy world he was creating in his mind was the country's true reality. He read anti-government literature associated with gun laws and conspiracy literature and convinced himself that the U.S. government would soon begin a secret operation to deprive its citizens of their basic rights. McVeigh referred to this as "The New World Order."[50] McVeigh traveled to gun shows all over the country. He was obsessed with learning everything he could about the nation's "war" against the second amendment. McVeigh's opinions were rigid and Martha Crenshaw comments on such a phenomenon stating, "theories of cognitive consistency indicate that individuals absorb only information that supports their beliefs, ignore disconfirming evidence, fail to recognize value conflicts, and neglect to reconsider decisions once they are reached."[51] McVeigh's travel to national gun shows gave him the opportunity to discuss political issues with a population of like-minded people. Gun shows attracted many right wing citizens who shared McVeigh's belief that the second amendment was under fire and that our

---

[49] Michel and Herbeck, *American Terrorist,* 118.

[50] Ibid., 180.

[51] Martha Crenshaw, "Decisions to use Terrorism: Psychological Constraints on Instrumental Reasoning," in *Social Movements and Violence: Participation in Underground Organizations*, ed. Donatella della Porta (Greenwich, CT: JAI Press, Inc), 35.

subversive government threatened to erode our rights. This served to feed McVeigh's anti-government beliefs and convince him that something had to be done to prevent the coming government assault. He also found he could make money at these shows so he decided to make them his primary source of income.

McVeigh became obsessed with the gun show culture. As he traveled the country attending gun shows, he sought out his old Army buddies Terry Nichols and Michael Fortier. McVeigh was making decent money selling survival gear, anti-government bumper stickers, and t-shirts, which financed his travel. He appreciated the two shared his negative opinions of the government and he viewed them as trustworthy confidants. Nichols and Fortier became as close to McVeigh as brothers. They would assist McVeigh in obtaining temporary employment while he was in town and they served as his sounding board when he wished to discuss his beliefs and concerns about the U.S. government.

D.   POLITICAL FACTORS THAT TURN MCVEIGH AGAINST THE STATE

Donatella della Porta pinpoints "encounters with an unfair state" as a key accelerant to radicalization and militarization in her book *Social Movements, Political Violence, and the State: A Comparative Analysis* that compares German and Italian terrorists when she states, "for both Italian and German activists, the death of fellow comrades—at the hand of the police or the fascists—acquired a highly symbolic value as an expression of the degeneration of the state."[52] Three events the U.S. government would execute between August 1992 and September 1994 would engender the same feelings in Tim McVeigh. These events would prove to McVeigh that his prediction of a U.S. government assault on basic citizen rights had commenced. McVeigh believed the citizens of his country simply did not understand the dangerous future aims of their government.

---

[52] Donatella Della Porta, *Social Movements, Political Violence, and the State: A Comparative Analysis* (Cambridge, UK: Cambridge University Press, 1995), 158.

The Ruby Ridge tragedy in August 21, 1992, caught McVeigh's paranoid attention. The Ruby Ridge debacle transpired after Randy Weaver sold sawed off shotguns to an undercover ATF agent he met at a white separatist meeting. The government charged Weaver with selling illegal firearms. Weaver was a no-show on his court date. He sent a letter to the U.S. Marshal's office, stating he would not obey the law. The Marshals set up observation on his property "in hopes of finding an opportunity to safely arrest."[53] After the Weaver's dog barked at the agents, alerting the Weavers to the government's presence on the family's property, a gun battle broke out. It did not end well for either side. The tragedy "ended in the deaths of a U.S. marshal, Weaver's wife and his 14-year-old son."[54] McVeigh was infuriated the government took such drastic action against the Weaver family. McVeigh later commented that:

> An American family was being treated like a dangerous drug gang, and for what? Exercising their right to bear arms? Nobody seemed to care. It was no wonder citizens' freedoms were being scraped away little by little—nobody gave a damn.[55]

To McVeigh, this was a stark example of the government beginning to slowly dissolve the second amendment. His anger was palpable.

The Waco standoff in February 1993 angered McVeigh more than any other incident. ATF agents served David Koresh, the leader of the radical religious group the Branch Davidians, a search warrant for a suspected weapons cache at his compound. Koresh was rightfully suspected of possessing illegal automatic rifles, incendiary devices, and explosives. The Branch Davidians refused to allow authorities to search the premises and a complicated and lengthy stand off ensued. McVeigh was so concerned with the standoff at the Branch Davidian compound that he drove from Michigan to Waco to see if he could help. "In March 1993, McVeigh was captured on film by Texas television KTVT, a CBS affiliate, sitting on the hood of his car just outside the Davidian

---

[53] Gordan Witkin, "The nightmare of Idaho's Ruby Ridge," *U.S. News and World Report,* September 11, 1995, 4.

[54] Ibid..
[55] Stickney, *All American Monster,* 148.

24

compound."[56] McVeigh had gone to protest the standoff and was selling bumper stickers that read "Is your church ATF approved?"[57] After a 51-day standoff with the FBI, "Federal agents began battering holes in the walls of the Branch Dravidians compound and spraying tear gas inside," prompting the Davidians to finally end it by setting their compound ablaze. "David Koresh and 76 followers died—including at least 17 children."[58] McVeigh, who was visiting his Army buddy Terry Nichols by this time, was outraged that the federal government would resort to such brutality. "The blaze at the Waco compound, more than any other single event, was the turning point in his life."[59] McVeigh was sure the government was responsible for the fire, the deaths and what he felt was an unwarranted ATF imposition on private citizens in the first place.

Finally, in September 1994, the United States Government passed the Federal Assault Weapons Ban. "The 1994 law banned the sale to civilians of 19 types of semiautomatic weapons, including semiautomatic versions of the Intratec Tec-9 pistol and Uzi submachine gun."[60] McVeigh interpreted this as a government ploy to criminalize gun owners. He thought this law would broaden the government's reach, allowing agents to legitimately arrest him and gun owners like him. It would make him a criminal overnight. Although McVeigh believed this, it was not true because the law banned the purchase of semiautomatic weapons from its activation date and did not penalize citizens who already owned such weapons. Nevertheless, McVeigh saw this as another step toward the New World Order, an attack on second amendment rights, and the total domination of the United States Government.

---

[56] Stickney, *All American Monster,* 154.

[57] Ibid.

[58] *Sam Verhovek, "*Death in Waco: Scores die as compound is set on fire as FBI send tanks in with Tear gas," *The New York Times,* April 20, 1993,1.

[59] Michel and Herbeck, *American Terrorist,* 161.

[60] Dan Eggen, "Enthusiasts Eye Assault Rifles as Ban Nears End; Report: Makers Taking Orders," *The Washington Post,* September 8, 2004, A3.

E. IDEOLOGICAL FACTORS; THE MOVE TO TERRORISM

One month after the siege at Waco, McVeigh declared war against his own country. He told his buddy Mike Fortier, "the time had come to take action against the government."[61] Once the Federal Assault Weapons Ban was passed, McVeigh began to plan how he would carry out his attack against the government. "It could be a fire bombing, a sniper attack, a kidnapping, an assassination, whatever it took."[62] He was determined to stand up to the federal government and avenge the injustices the government was causing. In his mind, the second amendment rights of all Americans would soon be completely taken away. He could not allow it to happen. He immersed himself in the gun show culture, attended militia, and religious extremist rallies, honed his skills as a shooter, and renewed his experimentation with homemade incendiary devices and bombs. He showed a new indifference to laws and began to commit petty thefts to make a couple extra dollars. McVeigh was convinced of the government plot to usher in the New World Order and that it was conducting secret operations against citizens all over the country. McVeigh even took a trip to "the mysterious Area 51 military installation in Roswell, New Mexico"[63] in the summer of 1994 to see if he could observe the compound in hope of discovering such a plot.

In close consultation with Terry Nichols, McVeigh decided to target a federal building. McVeigh planned the bombing to coincide with the second anniversary of the Waco siege. He believed this attack would effectively communicate his dissatisfaction with the U.S. government. After conducting extensive reconnaissance on his potential targets, McVeigh settled on the Alfred P. Murrah Federal Building in Oklahoma City, Oklahoma. The Murrah building housed a large number of government agencies; it was positioned well to minimize collateral damage to people outside the building who did not

---

[61] Michel and Herbeck, *American Terrorist,* 162.

[62] Ibid., 191.

[63] Ibid., 184. McVeigh visited Area 51 because he was paranoid there was a government conspiracy in the country. Ruby Ridge, Waco, and the Federal Assault Weapons Ban had convinced him that the New World Order was active and would strike at any moment. Maybe he could get a glimpse of the secretive New World Order preparing at Area 51. Area 51, an Air Force base in Nevada, has always been perceived by the American public as a secretive base that the government carries out its most important top secret missions. To McVeigh, Area 51 seemed like the ideal location for the secretive New World Order to be.

work for the government; and its vast proportions of glass promised it was structurally perfect to dramatically crumble under the blast of a bomb. Between October 1994 and April 1995 McVeigh and Nichols, with the knowledge of Fortier, collected the materials necessary to build their bomb. To obtain their materials, they would steal, buy, and travel great distances to acquire the necessary components. McVeigh was focused on the mission at hand, but was very paranoid his plot would be revealed. He wrote his sister in March 1995 saying that, "he feared 'G-men' might intercept his mail to her, or that if she sent him a letter, they might take it from his post office box in Arizona and incriminate her."[64] McVeigh's sister did not know exactly what her brother was up to; however, she knew enough to know he was up to no good.

McVeigh and Nichols had purchased all the components for the bomb with relative ease and at a small expense. All the components combined cost just under five thousand dollars. As McVeigh finalized his plans he sent his sister another letter and instructed her to keep it. McVeigh knew federal agents would find the letter in the investigation after the bombing if he were caught. It said:

> ATF: All you tyrannical motherfuckers will swing in the wind one day for your treasonous actions against the Constitution of the United States. Remember the Nuremberg War Trials. But...but...but... I only followed orders...Die, you spineless cowardice bastards.[65]

McVeigh also wrote a few other letters to friends and family that would later be deemed as goodbye letters. In his last letter to his little sister Jennifer, the letter concluded "won't be back forever."[66] He was prepared to give his life in his struggle against the government. McVeigh expected he had a good chance of being captured during, or immediately following, his attack.

Six months after planning and resourcing his attack, McVeigh began assembling his massive bomb. After renting a Ryder truck outside of Junction City, Kansas,

---

[64] Brandon Stickney, "Bombing suspect McVeigh a believer in strange government conspiracies," *The Skeptical Enquirer,* May/June 1997, 6.

[65] Michel and Herbeck, *American Terrorist,* 214.

[66] Jo Thomas, "McVeigh Described as Terrorist and as Victim of Circumstance," *New York Times,* May 30, 1997, 1.

McVeigh picked up the bomb components from the storage shed that he and Nichols had rented, and drove to Geary Lake outside Fort Riley, Kansas. McVeigh was familiar with the area because of the time he spent stationed there with the Army. On the night of April 18, 1995, McVeigh constructed his bomb. Early the next morning, after eating an Army Meal Ready to Eat (MRE), McVeigh began his drive to Oklahoma City. McVeigh treated the operation like a mission he would go on while in the military. He believed his mission would ultimately bring about more good than bad.

At 9:02AM on April 19, 1995, "the Alfred P. Murrah Federal Building in Oklahoma City, Oklahoma was bombed, resulting in the death of one hundred and sixty eight people, and injuring at least five hundred and nine others."[67] McVeigh would nearly escape from Oklahoma that day in the getaway car that he and Nichols had planted in OKC days earlier; however, he was pulled over on a routine traffic stop for not having a license plate on his car. After being pulled over, the officer noticed McVeigh had a pistol holstered, and immediately arrested him for carrying an unregistered firearm. It would be three days later, hours before McVeigh was to be released for these minor infractions, that the Federal Bureau of Investigation would realize they had the man responsible for the bombing already in custody.

F.   OKLAHOMA CITY BOMBING AFTERMATH

> On June 2, 1997, Timothy James McVeigh was convicted of eleven counts of murder and conspiracy resulting from his involvement in the Oklahoma City bombing. Two months later, he was sentenced to death on all eleven counts.[68]

McVeigh was incarcerated for over six years before he was put to death. In all of those six years, he never apologized for his actions, and he died believing the bombing had benefitted the country. Martha Crenshaw describes a terrorist's psychological justification to kill, stating they:

---

[67] Hammer and Paul, *Secrets Worth Dying For,* 20.

[68] Ibid.

tend to dehumanize any victims, accusing them of the crimes and outrages. Alternatively, targets are portrayed as being a structure or organization, not individual human beings with personal lives.[69]

This illustrates McVeigh's beliefs perfectly. The citizens who had died in the Murrah building worked for the government and were, therefore, complicit in the government's crimes. McVeigh had only one regret when it came to the bombing. He had been unaware there was a daycare on the premises, on the second floor of the Murrah building. He had neglected to enter the building during his reconnaissance, and that omission troubled him. McVeigh had dismissed the idea of bombing a federal building in Arkansas because it had stores on the first floor and he wished only to harm people directly connected to the government. McVeigh ultimately blamed the Murrah building bombing's 168 deaths on the federal government. After all, had the federal government not taken hostile action at Ruby Ridge and Waco, McVeigh would have never been moved to retaliate so dramatically.

While on death row, McVeigh was obsessed with his legacy and how the American public would perceive him after he was gone. He desperately wished for his biography *American Terrorist* to be published before his death. He believed that once the world read it, the reasons behind his attack would make sense to everyone. He would go down in history as a great American patriot like Alexander Hamilton or Thomas Paine. McVeigh wanted this so badly he was willing to sacrifice anything or anyone to maintain or improve his image. A fellow death row inmate, Juan Garza, was waiting to be put to death as the federal government's first capital punishment execution at the same time McVeigh was on death row. Garza was fighting the government in court to have his execution overturned. Garza and McVeigh knew each other well. All the death row inmates at the Federal Penitentiary in Terre Haute, Indiana agreed to be on their best behavior and grant no interviews that could negatively affect Garza's fight for life. McVeigh, only concerned for himself, scheduled a *60 Minutes* interview that would air one week prior to the court's ruling on Garza's appeal. Garza and his attorney pleaded

---

[69] Martha Crenshaw, *Encyclopedia of World Terrorism Volume II* (Armonk, New York: M.E. Sharpe Corp., 1997), 248.

with McVeigh to delay the interview until after Garza's appeal had been decided, but McVeigh refused. "When the CBS '60 Minutes' interview with McVeigh was aired in March 2000, the impact upon all federal death row inmates was immediate."[70] McVeigh came off as cold, calculating, and unforgiving in the interview. Members of Congress called for harsher capital punishment laws. All this press and attention rained down just before Garza's federal appeal decision would be handed down. McVeigh had little empathy for his fellow man, even in the last months of his life. Garza lost his appeal in court and would be put to death seven days after McVeigh.

G.   ANALYSIS OF TIM MCVEIGH

Timothy McVeigh was a consistently isolated person whose narcissistic delusions of grandeur drove him to impose his beliefs on an unsuspecting public in a most violent and dramatic way. From boyhood, he was left alone because his parents worked outside the home. McVeigh's interactions with his peers were difficult. He was intelligent, so he retreated to his imagination and perhaps he found it so comfortable there, he never fully reemerged. His fantasy world cast him as the victor, vigilante, and enforcer of a specific code of honor where he asked all the questions and supplied all the answers.

For years, he warred against an invisible enemy. The most positive and affirming interactions of his youth involved a gun-centered relationship with his grandfather. McVeigh learned guns made him feel good. The survivalist lifestyle appealed to him. He was affirmed by others, like him, preparing for an unknown battle. Maybe these preparations made him feel smart, purposeful. Every job McVeigh ever held involved guns. But he always felt marginalized when he interacted with mainstream society. He was an armored car guard, a rent-a-cop and he earned little money and even less respect. He could not get a date. He preferred seclusion most of the time. His few friends were just as delusional as he was. The one time he was successful within the mainstream culture, when he was a gunner in the Army, that success felt so foreign to him, he worried he had become one of "them," one of the enemies of childhood and imagination who had hounded him his whole life. He was on the dark side, bullying another country. So he

---

[70] Hammer and Paul, *Secrets Worth Dying For,* 127.

blew the biggest opportunity of his life, to become a Special Forces Operative, and fled back to obscurity where no one but him gave the orders. He returned to the gun culture, back to the beliefs that stoked his fantastical worldview. He traveled around the country, selling survivalist gear at gun shows and searching for signs. He read conspiracy theory documents and was a racist.

McVeigh believed the government bullied other nations aggressively. He believed the government was after the thinkers like him, the guys asking the big questions. He scoured the news for evidence of his enemy advancing, he listened to the rants of others who, like him, lived on the fringes. One day, he finally found the sign he told himself he had sought all along. He thought he saw our government do wrong, and with zeal, he studied Ruby Ridge, and he read some more. The nightmare at Waco stoked the fire McVeigh had longed to light his whole life. He traveled to Waco and sat near the standoff to show his solidarity. His life became one of traveling and seeking knowledge of the vast government cover-ups and conspiracies that threatened all right-thinking individuals, like him.

McVeigh's guns were so important that he felt the need to stockpile from a young age. The passing of the Assault Weapon Ban convinced McVeigh that the government had finally decided to turn his way of life into a criminal one. He became convinced that faceless enemy he had always feared truly was the federal government. He was bullied as a child, whispered about by his Army buddies and, ultimately, so imaginative that in the end he had a tough time separating truth from paranoia. McVeigh waged a war on our government, and ultimately forced his overblown image of himself on the world in a fiery explosion of glass and government workers. He finally completed something that cast him as the avenger. He had stood up to Goliath and taken a swing, all in the name of our Constitution. He believed he was an American hero, a great defender of the Constitution whose legacy would bear out the truth: If we stay silent, bad things happen. We get beaten up, our rights get eroded, we bomb nations unable to defend themselves.

McVeigh had no empathy for anyone unless they fit into the narrow confines of his political ideology. He never meant to harm the children in the Murrah Building, but still, he called the victims collateral damage. Even at the end, McVeigh was concerned

31

the masses did not see him in the hero role. He wanted to leave his legacy and cared deeply how he would be remembered. By the end, he was, again, willing to sacrifice others, in this case, his fellow death row inmate and friend, in order to preserve his legacy as someone who stood up and defended himself and all lovers of the Constitution. He went to the death chair never wavering from his rigid ideology. He believed the book *American Terrorist* would tell his side of the story and the American public would finally understand. He identified with the isolated child, the kitten in the bag, and the citizen in peril who was willing to don the cape of heroism and risk it all for his cause and for the nation he professed to love. McVeigh's ideology got all tangled up within his imagination, his delusions, and his narcissistic personality; these made him nothing more than an ineffectual, loathsome, lone wolf terrorist.

III.   TED KACZYNSKI: PATTERNS OF RADICALIZATION

Theodore Kaczynski stands as the smartest, most educated, and most elusive domestic lone wolf terrorist in our nation's history. His infamous terrorist acts involve assembling and mailing bombs to numerous universities and airlines. The FBI combined the first three letters of the words that represent his targets: UN (University) and A (Airlines) to dub him "The Unabomber." Kaczynski began his terrorist campaign in 1978 in hopes of ushering in a revolution that would alert society to the dangers of both technological advancement and industrialization. He believed the rapid advancement of the industrial revolution and technology in the United States was destroying our society. He targeted symbols of innovation and progress. It would take the Federal Bureau of Investigation nearly 18 years, 1978–1996, to capture him. During his terrorist campaign, Kaczynski's "16 bomb attacks killed 3 people and wounded 29 more."[71] Prior to his capture, he would also publish his manifesto detailing his vision of future society.

A.   CHILDHOOD AND UPBRINGING

Ted Kaczynski was born on May 22, 1942 to a Polish, agnostic, working class family in Chicago. Ted's father Turk owned a local meat store and his mother, Wanda, was a homemaker. Although Ted's parents were working class, they were both intellectually gifted and valued education and academic advancement above all else.

> In only one way was the Kaczynski household unusual: in its intense intellectuality. This would become the leitmotif in Ted's life. From the beginning, Turk and Ted's intellectual interests would isolate the family from its neighbors and Ted from his peers. As the son grew older, his preoccupation with books and ideas would loom even larger, until it created a social gulf too wide for him to cross.[72]

Ted's father put him under intense academic pressure starting in elementary school. Turk, who had his own problems including depression and bitterness toward his life,

---

[71] David Streitfeld, "Kaczynski, in Book, Says He's not Crazy," *The Washington Post,* February 12, 1999, C2.

[72] Alston Chase, *A Mind For Murder* (New York: W.W. Norton & Company, 2004), 161.

verbally abused Ted often. "When Turk got angry at Ted, he would accuse him of being insane, or psychotic, using these words not in their clinical sense but merely as terms of derision."[73]

Kaczynski was shy, struggling to fit in and make friends in elementary school. He immersed himself in books to escape the extreme academic pressure and verbal abuse. Kaczynski was not viewed negatively by his classmates, though, and felt his life was pretty normal until his fifth-grade year. His school identified him as a gifted student; they administered an IQ test "on which he achieved a 'genius' score of 167."[74] He was forced to skip the sixth grade. Kaczynski's life changed drastically when he reached the seventh grade. He was significantly smaller than the other boys, who treated him as an outcast.

> He would never be accepted by his new classmates, who were at least a year older. The bigger boys bullied and teased him. The girls ignored him. He sank to the lowest social level, where he remained.[75]

Ted isolated himself and focused in on the only thing he had left: academics. "While his younger brother David played ball with other kids, Ted huddled in the attic with his arithmetic, a hermit at 11."[76]

B.   EDUCATION, TRAINING, AND THE FOUNDATIONS OF IDEOLOGY

Kaczynski became accustomed to his role as an outsider, a social outcast. "Kaczynski's family has said he was always an antisocial child and that his behavior got worse as he got older."[77] His parents dialed up the academic pressure as he advanced through grade levels. As if Ted had not endured enough complication due to the age and maturity gaps between himself and his classmates, his school recommended he skip his junior year of high school as well. His parents did him no favors by jumping at the

---

[73] Chase, *A Mind For Murder,* 162.

[74] Ibid., 163.

[75] Ibid.

[76] Anonymous, "Theodore Kaczynski," *People Weekly,* December 30, 1996, 52.

[77] David Jackson, "Man behind the mask," *TIME,* November 17, 1997, 51.

opportunity. They thought they were furthering his education when, in reality, they were simply fueling his sense of isolation from society. As a 15-year-old senior in high school, Ted faced enormous amounts of ridicule and teasing from his classmates. Due to his age and maturity level, he was "incapable of attracting female companionship."[78] He was alone and bitter; his studies were his only salvation. Kaczynski's academic prowess got him admitted to Harvard, where he was introduced into a culture of elite, privileged kids with little tolerance for a 16-year-old, blue-collar freshman.

Kaczynski's isolationism was not out of the ordinary at Harvard. It was common for students to become so involved and overwhelmed with their studies that they would spend most of their time in their rooms alone. This environment transformed Kaczynski. Although still on the social fringe, he would not be as noticed, teased or ostracized at Harvard. The Harvard culture dovetailed nicely with his solitary mode of operation but his antisocial bent did not go wholly unnoticed.

> At Harvard, where he studied math, housemates recalled him as the guy whose room was sour-smelling and who fled from human contact. As one of them, astronomer Patrick McIntosh, recalled, Ted had a special talent for avoiding relationships by moving quickly past groups of people and slamming the door behind him.[79]

When Kaczynski entered Harvard, an educational revolution had just been completed. Harvard had instituted a new curricular general education program that all undergraduates would take beginning in the late 1940s. The curriculum was well-rehearsed and fully implemented when Kaczynski stepped on campus in 1958. "By 1958, when Mr. Kaczynski arrived at Harvard as an undergraduate, the cold war had created covert new links between research and government, links calling for moral blinders that rendered traditional scientific ethics all but obsolete."[80] For a young, immature, teenage Kaczynski, the education he would receive through the new general education program would set the foundations for his ideology. Alston Chase, author of

---

[78] Chase, *A Mind For Murder,* 178.

[79] Anonymous, "Theodore Kaczynski," 52–53.

[80] Janet Maslin, "The Unabomber and the 'Culture of Despair'," *New York Times,* March 3, 2003, E10.

the book *A Mind For Murder* and undergraduate at Harvard from 1953 to 1957, discusses the effect the general education program had on students like him.

> Gen Ed delivered to those of us who were undergraduates during this time a double whammy of pessimism. From humanists we learned that science threatens civilization. From the scientists we learned that science couldn't be stopped. Taken together, they implied there is no hope. Gen Ed had created what would become a permanent fixture at Harvard, and indeed, throughout academe: the culture of despair.[81]

Kaczynski studied and read, fervently locking himself in his room for hours at a time and only emerging when absolutely necessary. For Ted is would be "the intellectual 'culture of despair' that characterized Ivy League academe at that time and that seems to have influenced the isolated and gnomic Kaczynski"[82] that would set his life on a downward spiral.

Kaczynski experienced another life-altering event at Harvard in his dealings with a psychology professor, Dr. Henry Murray. Professor Murray was running a controversial psychological experiment at Harvard called the "Multiform Assessments of Personality Development among Gifted College Men."[83] The professor "recruited the future Unabomber for a psychological experiment with 'Manchurian Candidate' overtones."[84] Kaczynski volunteered to be a participant in the experiment to earn himself extra money. "Murray's preliminary screening would identify him as the most alienated of the entire cohort."[85] He would spend 200 hours as a subject participating within the experiment over his sophomore and junior year.

> The experiments involved what Murray called 'stressful disputation' or 'the Dyad,' but 'whatever its name, it was a highly refined version of the third degree.' Subjects like Mr. Kaczynski were humiliated, ridiculed, and secretly photographed while debating overqualified opponents.[86]

---

[81] Chase, *A Mind For Murder,* 206.

[82] Alan Judd, "Method in his Madness," *The Spectator,* September 6, 2003, 46.

[83] Chase, *A Mind For Murder,* 229.

[84] Maslin, "The Unabomber and the Culture of Despair," E10.

[85] Chase, *A Mind For Murder,* 230.

[86] Maslin, "The Unabomber and the Culture of Despair," E10.

Obviously, Kaczynski did not know the purpose of the experiments; however; the experience fostered within him a lasting animosity toward psychologists. "As he continued to suffer through Murray's experiments, Kaczynski began to worry about society's use of mind control."[87]

During Kaczynski's senior year at Harvard, he began to recognize his feelings of loathing toward his personal situation and hate toward society. He "put together a theory to explain his unhappiness and anger: Technology and science were destroying liberty."[88] Kaczynski had merged all he had learned through the Harvard curriculum of despair and the horrible experience he had within Murray's experiment. His education at Harvard was quickly planting the seeds of Kaczynski's future psyche and ideology. In his book *The Terrorist*, Maxwell Taylor, a renowned psychologist states, "The experience of university itself gives rise to the questioning of society's values universities certainly have proved to be ideological training grounds for many terrorists."[89] Everything he had believed important, like mathematics, at which he was brilliant, was simply stressed to improve the government's system, and he believed the system was at the very heart of everything that was wrong with society. "Bit by bit, society—the system—was destroying him."[90] Kaczynski would graduate from Harvard in 1962 and attend the University of Michigan for graduate school.

Kaczynski continued his education in mathematics at the University of Michigan, even though he had begun to despise it because of its direct effect on the advancement of technology in society. He continued to study mathematics because it was all he had. Kaczynski's dissertation was awarded the "Mathematical Department's Summer Myers Prize as the most outstanding doctoral dissertation of 1967."[91] His dissertation had solved a math problem that the Professors at the University of Michigan presented to their students for years claiming it unsolvable; Kaczynski solved it within a few weeks of

[87] Todd Gitlin, "A Dangerous Mind," *The Washington Post,* March 2, 2003, 6.

[88] Chase, *A Mind For Murder,* 293.

[89] Maxwell Taylor, *The Terrorist* (London: Brassey's Defence Publishers, 1988), 127.

[90] Chase, *A Mind For Murder,* 292.

[91] Ibid., 301.

receiving the challenge. The issue for Kaczynski was that the mathematical work he was completing was so cutting-edge that only a few people in the world were smart enough to understand its significance.

Kaczynski's lifestyle habits did not change at the University of Michigan. He still lived as a reclusive loner, was dateless, and suspected others despised him, although he continued to complete amazing, cutting-edge work in mathematics in his program. It was at Michigan where Kaczynski would experience his first thoughts of killing in order to get even with society. It began one night when a sleepless Kaczynski could hear his neighbors having sex. The sound of sex maddened him because of its inaccessibility. Years of solitude had embittered Kaczynski. He began to have crazy thoughts that he would do anything to be with a woman, even become one. He decided to get a sex change operation after concluding, "only by becoming a woman could he hope to touch one."[92]

After making an appointment at a health clinic in the hopes of scheduling a sex change operation, Kaczynski decided not to go through with it at the last second. To do so, he would have been forced to talk to a psychologist, and he feared what the psychologist would do or say to him. He despised psychologists and realized this one would be no different than the one who impacted him so negatively at Harvard. He was ashamed that he had nearly embarrassed himself at the clinic. He despised himself for almost letting a psychologist back into his life. He had reached a desperate point in his life. A point that he fantasized about what it would be like to kill.

Kaczynski was tired of following the rules of society that had benefitted him so little. "He resolved to ignore the strictures of society and do only what he wanted."[93] He would now follow his own rules. In his journal, recovered after his capture, he had recorded an entry on Christmas 1972 that read:

> About a year and a half ago, I planned to murder a scientist—as a means of revenge against organized society in general, and the technological establishment in particular. Unfortunately, I chickened out. I couldn't

---

[92] Chase, *A Mind For Murder,* 305.

[93] Ibid., 306.

work up the nerve to do it. . . . My plan was such that there was very little chance of my getting caught. I had no qualms before I tried to do it, and I thought I would have no difficulty. I had everything well prepared.[94]

The seeds of revenge had been planted. Ted would graduate from the University of Michigan and take a job as a professor at U.C. Berkeley in 1966. As he was headed to Berkeley, his decision to seek revenge on society had already been made. Kaczynski's "decision to leave academe was made in Michigan that fateful fall of 1966, as he left the University Health Center psychiatrist's office."[95] Berkeley was simply a necessary step to gain the financing he would need to carry out his plans.

C. FROM LOCAL CRIMINAL TO TERRORIST

Kaczynski taught at U.C. Berkeley for only three years before leaving in 1969. He accepted the Berkeley job to bankroll his escape from society. Once he left, it would take Ted over a year and a half to finally settle in Montana. In 1971, Ted bought land and a cabin in Lincoln, Montana. He was excited and knew it would be in Montana where his revenge fantasies would become actual terror plots. There was no one to bother him, and no one to answer to; he had created his own world. In April 1971, Kaczynski wrote in his journal:

> My motive for doing what I am going to do is simply personal revenge. I do not expect to accomplish anything by it. Of course, if my crime gets any public attention, it may help to stimulate public interest in the technology question, and thereby improve the chances of stopping technology before it is too late; but, on the other hand, most people will probably be repelled by my crime, and the opponents of freedom may use it as a weapon to support their arguments for control of human behavior.[96]

Kaczynski could go weeks without human contact at his cabin; he had never been happier. He loved the freedom that his newfound solitude afforded him. This environment of isolation and loneliness "focuses the terrorist within a political context

---

[94] Sara Van Boven and Patricia King, "A killer's self-portrait," *Newsweek,* May 11, 1998, 38.

[95] Chase, *A Mind For Murder,* 309.

[96] Chris Waits and Dave Shors, *UNABOMBER: The Secret Life of Ted Kaczynski* (Helena: Helena Independent Record and Montana Magazine, 1999), 264–265.

and confirms his marginal states in society, imposing a natural limit and constraint on the scope of terrorist action."[97] Kaczynski had plenty of constraints, living, as he was, in the woods with no steady income. He would spend four years at his cabin before he would make his move toward terrorist activities. Richard Clutterbuck describes the process and timeline of radicalization when an individual goes from a peaceful protestor to killer describing members of the Baader-Meinhof gang in his book *The Future of Political Violence.* He states, "The development from peaceful protest to terrorism is a gradual one…Those who did graduate to cold-blooded killing did so over the years in a process of escalation fueled by frustration."[98] Kaczynski's would follow the same path of escalation in the forest on Montana.

Kaczynski began to act on his frustrations in 1975. He felt he was not isolated enough and was discouraged by the substantial hustle and bustle around his home. He trekked deep into the woods to build a secret cabin.

> He built his remote structure so he could get away from noise and people, but he also used it and its secret location to plan and plot his acts of murder and revenge…he also had a refuge where he could sometimes build and test his bombs.[99]

This was a significant marker in his pattern of radicalization. Once the secret cabin was built, Kaczynski would begin executing criminal acts in his area.

He would commit a number of local criminal acts before launching his first terrorist attack in 1978. Kaczynski began setting booby traps in the woods surrounding his cabin. He was angry at a recent uptick in motorcycle and bike use on the trails in the woods. Chris Waits, co-author of *UNABOMBER: The Secret Life of Ted Kaczynski* lived within a mile of Kaczynski in Lincoln and owned a large portion of the local land. He came into contact with one of Ted's first traps while on a hike.

---

[97] H.H.A. Cooper, "What is a Terrorist: A Psychological Prospective," *Legal Medical Quarterly* (1977): 16, quoted in Taylor, *The Terrorist,* 129.

[98] Richard Clutterbuck, *The Future of Political Violence: Destabilization, Disorder, and Terrorism* (New York: St. Martin's Press, 1986), 22.

[99] Waits and Shors, *UNABOMBER,* 166–167.

> A half pace away was a small but strong wire stretched across the trail at neck height in a most dangerous place…The deadly trap was strategically placed where it would be impossible to steer a bike quickly to clear, even if the rider saw the wire.[100]

Kaczynski used neck wires as his first means to kill. He knew the probability of killing with one of his wires was slim, however, it was an important step within his radicalization process. In Ted's journal he commented, "At the end of summer '75 after the roaring by of motorcycles near my camp spoiled a hike for me, I put a piece of wire across a trail where cycle tracks were visible, at about neck height for a motorcycle."[101]

Between the summer of 1975 and May of 1978, when he built and delivered his first bomb, he would continue to execute local criminal acts and experiment with explosives at his secret cabin. His criminal acts became progressively more pointed and dangerous as time went on. He had come to his remote retreat in Lincoln to get away from society, but it seemed he could not escape it.

> He was already acutely sensitive to noise, and had discovered there was plenty in his new neighborhood. The sounds of chain saws, snowmobiles, jet planes, prospectors, and helicopters drove him to new heights of rage.[102]

He warred against anyone who came into the area, especially if that person brought in anything technology-related. In 1977, a minor came to the area to do some work and brought excavation equipment with him. He came to his site one day and found "someone had trashed his cabin, vandalized his small bulldozer and stolen its magneto so the dozer wouldn't run."[103] Kaczynski would commit multiple local crimes like this one as he prepared to take the next step in his campaign; a step that would take him from a local criminal to a terrorist.

---

[100] Waits and Shors, *UNABOMBER,*, 84–85.

[101] Ibid., 206.

[102] Chase, *A Mind For Murder,* 337.

[103] Waits and Shors, *UNABOMBER,* 86.

D.   KACZYNSKI THE TERRORIST

In 1978, Kaczynski morphed from a criminal who dreamed of exacting revenge on society, to a terrorist possessing the expertise, will, and tools to do it. Kaczynski had a clear picture of his targets in mind. In a journal entry from fall 1977, he stated:

> The technological society may be in some sense inevitable, but it is so only because of the way people behave. Consequently, I hate people...of course, the people I hate most are those who consciously and willfully promote the technological society, such as scientists, big businessmen, union leaders, politicians, etc.[104]

Kaczynski would refer to his bombs in his journal as a series of numbered experiments. He treated his bombings more like a series of science experiments than terrorist acts. This helped take the human dimension out of the equation. Cindy Combs discusses this concept in her book *Terrorism in the Twenty-First Century*. She states that for a terrorist:

> The enemy is viewed in depersonalized and monolithic terms, as capitalist, communist, the bourgeoisie, or imperialist. It is not human beings whom the terrorist fights; rather, it is this dehumanized monolith.[105]

Kaczynski believed he was superior to everyone else. He tended to view the people around him as diminished in their capacities to understand their environments. In an undated journal entry he stated he was a "particularly important person and superior to most of the rest of the human race."[106] The rules did not apply to him because of his unique perspective; the rest of the public simply did not grasp it. Cindy Combs again weighs in on this belief stating:

> Revolutionary terrorists seem to view themselves as above the prevailing morality, as morally superior. Normal standards of behavior do not apply to them. They do not deem themselves in any sense as bound by conventional laws or conventional morality, which they often regard as the corrupt and self-serving tool of the enemy.[107]

---

[104] Waits and Shors, *UNABOMBER,* 269.

[105] Cindy Combs, *Terrorism in the Twenty-First Century: Fourth Edition* (Saddle River, NJ: Pearson Education, Inc., 2006), 44.

[106] Chase, *A Mind For Murder,* 329.

[107] Combs, *Terrorism in the Twenty-First Century,* 45.

Kaczynski executed his first major terrorist attack on May 25, 1978 targeting a scientist at Northwestern University. This bomb would injure a security guard. Shortly following his first attempt he decided to blow up an airplane. On 15 November 1979, Kaczynski:

> Shipped a package containing an explosive device, and it was triggered in flight. The bomb failed to explode, but it did generate large quantities of smoke. The crew diverted to Dulles Airport near Washington and landed without further incident. All six crew members and 72 passengers survived, though 12 passengers suffered from smoke inhalation.[108]

After the airlines bombing in 1979, Kaczynski would launch nine additional mail bomb attacks between 1979 and 1987 killing one and wounding six. He genuinely did not feel empathy for his victims. He wrote in his journal:

> I'll just chuck all of this silly morality business and hate anybody I please. Since then I have never had any interest in or respect for morality, ethics, or anything of the sort.[109]

Although Kaczynski had experienced some limited success with the lethality of his bombs, he was frustrated that the majority of his devices were too weak to kill. He stated in an undated section of his journal:

> May 1982, I sent a bomb to a computer expert named Patrick Fischer. His secretary opened it. One newspaper said she was in hospital? In good condition? With arm and chest cuts. Other newspaper said bomb drove fragments of wood into her flesh. But no indication that she was permanently disabled. Frustrating that I can't seem to make a lethal bomb. Used shotgun powder in this last hoping it would do better than rifle powder x x x Revenge attempts have been gobbling much time, impeding other work. But I must succeed, must get revenge.[110]

This is what made Kaczynski so dangerous as a bomb maker and terrorist. He was never satisfied with his work. He made each component of his bombs by hand with extreme attention to detail and steadily improved their lethality through the years.

---

[108] Air Safe Public Information, "Fatal Plane Crashes and Significant Events for the Boeing 727," Air Safe, http://www.airsafe.com/events/models/b727.htm.

[109] Waits and Shors, *UNABOMBER,* 267.

[110] "Excerpts From the Unabomber's Journal," *The New York Times*, April 29, 1998, 18.

As his bombs became more powerful, Mr. Kaczynski's coldness toward his victims grew more apparent. After his first deadly attack in 1985 in Sacramento killed Hugh Scrutton, the owner of a computer rental store, Mr. Kaczynski wrote: 'Excellent. Humane way to eliminate somebody. He probably never felt a thing.[111]

Frederick Hacker, a psychologist from the University of Southern California participating in a panel discussion in the book *The Rationalization of Terrorism* discusses the psyche of a terrorist while killing. He cites a French terrorist named Henri who had committed a bombing of a café in Paris that killed people.

> The innocence of the victims is indeed irrelevant for the terrorist, but then he feels that society by its injustice also punishes innocents without even recognizing that society's victims are indeed victimized…The essential aloneness of the terrorist is at least counter-matched in his fantasy by his conviction of speaking and acting for a group and for a higher, more sensitive form of universal justice.[112]

On February 20, 1987, Kaczynski was seen placing a bomb outside a computer store in Salt Lake City, Utah that would later injure the storeowner. The famous composite sketch of the Unabomber was created and released by the FBI. The composite sketch scared Kaczynski so he went back to Montana and did not bomb again for nearly seven years. During this break from his bombing attacks he resorted to stepping up local criminal acts around his home and work on making his bombs more lethal. "By the summer of 1992, after much experimentation at his secret wilderness testing sites, Kaczynski had developed the 'perfect detonator'."[113] His bombs were more powerful and more lethal than they had ever been. Armed with his new technology, he returned to bombing in 1993, launching four attacks between 1993 and 1995 killing two and seriously injuring two.

---

[111] David Johnston, "In Unabomber's Own Words, A Chilling Account of Murder," *The New York Times*, April 29, 1998, 1.

[112] David Rapoport and Yonah Alexander, *The Rationalization of Terrorism* (Frederick, MD: University Publications of America, Inc., 1982), 33.

[113] Chase, *A Mind For Murder,* 354–355.

Kaczynski would send his manifesto to the *New York Times* and the *Washington Post* in June 1995 in hopes of inspiring the American people to start the revolution against industrialized society he envisioned.

> In an April letter to the Times, the Unabomber said he would renounce terrorism—which he defined as 'intended to cause injury or death to human beings'—if his manuscript were published. But he reserved the right to engage in sabotage intended to destroy property without injuring human beings.[114]

The newspapers agreed to publish his manifesto, which ultimately led to his capture. Kaczynski's younger brother, David, was familiar with Ted's beliefs and writings, and he recognized his brother in the manifesto.

> The manifesto contained phrases and ideas that were similar to things Ted had penned over the years. 'Cool-headed logicians'—David remembered that phrase from one of Ted's letters.[115]

David turned his brother in. The FBI arrested Ted Kaczynski on April 3, 1996. He had eluded the authorities for almost 18 years.

E.   IDEOLOGY OF THE UNABOMBER

Ted Kaczynski is up front with his ideology in his manifesto. He believes "the industrial revolution and its consequences have been a disaster for the human race; the continued development of technology will worsen the situation."[116] He calls for a:

> Revolution against the industrial system…This is not to be a POLITICAL revolution. Its object will be to overthrow not governments but the economic and technological basis of the present society.[117]

---

[114] Chase, *A Mind For Murder,* 365.

[115] Serge F. Kovaleski, "His Brother's Keeper; When David Kaczynski let the FBI know that his older brother might be the Unabomber, he knew he was doing the right thing. But it's still hard to live with," *The Washington Post,* July 15, 2001, 10.

[116] Theodore Kaczynski, *The Unabomber Manifesto: Industrial Society & Its Future* (Minneapolis, Minnesota: Filiquarian Publishing, LLC, 1998), 5–6.

[117] Ibid., 6.

He believed the average citizen needed to wake up before it was too late. Kaczynski's manifesto insisted that the public must hear the earth's cry for rescue, and put an end to the industrial system in our country. He believed modern science could not be allowed to advance any further than it had already and the destruction of the industrial-technological system would benefit mankind. Only by returning to our 'wild nature' can we save ourselves, he believed. "Factories should be destroyed, technical books burned."[118] In essence, the world needed to reverse the momentum of industrialized society and work to get back to a pre-industrialized era.

Kaczynski truly believed that by publishing his manifesto in the *New York Times* and the *Washington Post* he had a chance to make a difference and start a revolution. He had many influences both on his ideology as a whole and on writing his manifesto, however; none was more important than a book written by sociologist Jacques Ellul entitled *The Technological Society*[119]. Kaczynski internalized the idea that society was unable to keep pace with technological advances and that the country was unraveling, on a collision course. Brother David "told the FBI, Ellul's Technological Society had become Ted's 'Bible'."[120] Ellul, like Kaczynski, worried that technology would be, in the end, be the downfall of society. Additionally, Joseph Conrad's book *The Secret Agent* had a profound impact on Kaczynski's ideology. In each bomb Kaczynski constructed he included a metal plate with the initials FC. Kaczynski got the idea from the book. In *The Secret Agent,* there was an "anarchist group, FP, or Future of the Proletariat."[121] He was so fascinated with the story that he got the idea for the name of his own group, Freedom Club or FC. He used the initials FC in each of his bombs, and when he wrote the *New York Times* and the *Washington Post,* before they published his manifesto. By saying he was the leader of the group FC, it gave the perception that a larger movement existed in the United States that thought as he did.

---

[118] "Excerpts From the Unabomber's Journal," *The New York Times*, 18.

[119] Jacques Ellul, *The Technological Society* (New York: Vintage Books, 1967).

[120] Chase, *A Mind For Murder,* 332.

[121] Ibid., 62.

Kaczynski's manifesto had been made available to millions after its publishing in the press. Kaczynski had succeeded in getting his message out to the bourgeoisie. Martha Crenshaw comments on the advantages of terrorism in the book *Origins of Terrorism: Psychologies, Ideologies, Theologies, and State of Mind.* She states in her chapter:

> Terrorism has an extremely useful agenda-setting function. If the reasons behind violence are skillfully articulated, terrorism can put the issue of political change on the public agenda. By attracting attention it makes the claims of the resistance a salient issue in the public mind.[122]

Kaczynski's journal was a huge find for the FBI. It admitted to, discussed, and analyzed each of his crimes and daily thoughts, and did so chronologically from 1972–1996. "In explaining his motives for murder, his journal did, indeed, move fluidly between citations of his twin desires of 'personal revenge' and to 'revenge against the system'."[123]

F.   ANALYSIS OF TED KACZYNSKI

Neglect, isolation and a prevalent sense of disapproval characterized Kaczynski's early home life. Later, he directed those very sentiments toward universities and airlines, which he blamed for all that ailed America. His father verbally abused him and repeatedly delivered the message that Kaczynski's academic achievement was all that mattered. Similarly, Kaczynski wrote a manifesto that detailed the faults of America's current course, and identified the institutions that pushed her too hard and, ultimately, would cause her failure. If only America could embrace its pre-Industrial revolution roots; if only America could untangle herself from the siren call of technology, he argued. Just as Kaczynski himself had been raced through his life, forced to skip ahead in school, left to contend with the devastating social and emotional consequences of decisions he was helpless to alter, he believed America was barreling toward an ill-defined fate at the

---

[122] Martha Crenshaw, "The logic of Terrorism: Terrorist behavior as a product of strategic choice," in *Origins of Terrorism: Psychologies, Ideologies, Theologies, States of Mind,* ed. Walter Reich (Washington D.C.: Woodrow Wilson Center Press, 1990), 17.

[123] Chase, *A Mind For Murder,* 341.

hands of harsh ideologues. So he would do them one better. He would strike back, crafting a detailed vendetta and lying patiently in wait with a blunt and blinding force he considered untraceable, unstoppable and unbeatable.

Did Kaczynski wish someone had paced his development and speed, as he was so fiercely determined to pace the way his nation grew up? Did he believe America mirrored his own promise and his own devastation? The desire to identify an external locus of control was strong with Kaczynski, who continually justified his beliefs and actions through his writings. He carefully planned his strikes against the institutions and symbols he felt were destroying our country. He had the patience to bide his time because his revenge was all he had left to offer the world. His hate and anger, stemming from his own life's circumstances, boiled over. He developed an extremist ideology to make sense out of his own isolation and despair. He blamed those who pushed America to achieve more, to be better, for all of her ills. He knew all about those who pushed for more, for better. Kaczynski had lived it. However, he was no longer a child, forced to allow others to dictate his trajectory. Kaczynski internalized the idea that society was unable to keep pace with technological advances and that the country was under siege.

Kaczynski strove to chart a revolution and to lead America off her destructive path. He built bombs and, true to his university background, cataloged them as if they were part of a research project. Kaczynski documented his every move, thoroughly. He even found a way to get his ideology out in front of the American public, which he considered a significant step toward achieving the social change he was willing to kill and maim to achieve. *The New York Times* and *The Washington Post* published his writings, under threat of his exacting further bomb plots upon unsuspecting institutions, and it was that mainstream exposure that finally halted his twisted quest to save his country.

As he alluded to in his journal, Kaczynski had two purposes in seeking his revenge. Revenge for personal reasons and revenge against the system as a whole. The system had turned him into the man he was. A loner, a man without female companionship, a man who contemplated turning himself into a woman to satisfy his desire to be with one, and a man who gave his all to succeed in the system rising to the

48

top of his field, mathematics, only to eventually dissolve into the forests of Montana and ultimately fail. If the system failed Kaczynski, the system had to be flawed and would ultimately fail society. He felt he was someone special, able to see the disaster society had looming in the fore that his fellow citizens could not perceive. As he radicalized in the forest he, like Timothy McVeigh, began to see himself as a leader, foot soldier, and secretary of a revolutionary movement. He would never waver from his rigid ideological beliefs. To this day Kaczynski sits in his cell at the Supermax prison in Florence, CO and continues to communicate his message to all who will listen. In the end, Kaczynski's heroism is palpable only to himself—he is simply a revolutionary lone wolf terrorist, plotting evil from the shadows of isolation.

THIS PAGE INTENTIONALLY LEFT BLANK

IV.   ERIC RUDOLPH: PATTERNS OF RADICALIZATION

Eric Rudolph is considered one of the most prolific domestic lone wolf terrorists in U.S. history. This chapter will examine Rudolph's life and chronicle his descent into radicalization. Rudolph morphed from an intelligent, religious, lower middle-class citizen into a radical lone wolf domestic terrorist responsible for the deaths of three Americans and the wounding of over 120 others. The study of Rudolph's pattern of radicalization and his associated ideological beliefs, psychology, attributes, traits, training, and education is relevant to our understanding of why he executed his deadly attacks and how we as a country can prevent future attacks. Rudolph is most infamous for bombing Centennial Olympic Park on July 27, 1996 during the Olympic Games in Atlanta. Additionally, Rudolph bombed abortion clinics in both Sandy Springs, Alabama, on January 16, 1997 and Birmingham, Alabama, on January 29, 1998, and an Atlanta lesbian bar on February 21, 1997.

A.   CHILDHOOD AND UPBRINGING

Eric Rudolph was born September 19, 1966 in Merritt Island, Florida as the fifth of six children in a lower middle-class family. Rudolph reportedly does not have bad memories of his childhood. After his capture, in an interview with Maryanne Vollers, author of *Lone Wolf: Murder, Myth, and the Pursuit of an American Outlaw*, Rudolph reflected on his childhood stating:

> We were a typical middle-class family. We had six children altogether, so the budget was tight. Despite the lack of material wealth, my parents were able to meet our basic needs.[124]

Robert Rudolph, Eric's father, an Army Veteran of both Korea and Vietnam, spent the majority of his life as an aircraft mechanic, while his mother, Patricia Rudolph, was deeply involved with religion. "As a young woman, she entered a Catholic convent

---

[124] Maryanne Vollers, *Lone Wolf: Murder, Myth, and the Pursuit of an American Outlaw* (New York: HarperCollins Publishers, 2006), 238.

and became a novice, the first step toward becoming a nun. She left before her final vows."[125] Religion would dominate Patricia's life as she struggled to identify a religion that suited her needs.

Eric Rudolph's mother influenced his belief patterns and future actions in a significant way. When she married his father in 1956, Patricia was active in the Catholic Workers group.

[The Catholic Workers were] committed to nonviolence, voluntary poverty, prayer, and hospitality for the homeless, exiled, hungry, and forsaken. Catholic Workers protest injustice, war, racism, and violence of all forms.[126]

Patricia participated in numerous protests and even moved to Washington, D.C. for a couple months to protest the atomic bomb in the U.S weapons arsenal. She stated, "We would have prayer vigils outside the White House and carry signs. Then in my spare time I'd sell the Catholic Worker newspaper on the corner."[127] At the time, "the FBI considered the Catholic Workers a subversive group and kept a thick file on the movement."[128] The Catholic Workers organization deeply moved Patricia Rudolph and harbored in her feelings of anger and mistrust of the federal government. She stated, "Those were exciting days ...We had meetings every week where different anarchists and pacifists would come and talk."[129] Patricia "described herself as 'a pacifist', an 'anarchist', 'anti-government, and a Christian.'"[130] She was a steadfast Pro Lifer and she struggled to find her brand of religion, spanning Catholic, Pentecostal, Evangelical, 7th Day Adventist, and finally, and most damaging, both the Christian Identity Movement and the Church of Israel all while taking care of a very young Eric. One thing was certain, Patricia's deep religious beliefs would be passed down to her son.

---

[125] Kathleen Walls, *Man Hunt: The Eric Rudolph Story* (LaVergne, TN: Global Authors Publications, 2003), 5.

[126] The Catholic Worker Movement, "Celebrating 75 Years 1933–2008," Catholic Worker, http://www.catholicworker.org/index.cfm.

[127] Vollers, *Lone Wolf,* 245.

[128] Ibid.

[129] Ibid.

[130] Walls, *Man Hunt,* 5.

Patricia Rudolph's religious zeal and unusual misgivings about the powers that be set the stage for her son's extraordinarily offbeat adolescence. Maryanne Vollers interviewed Patricia Rudolph following her son's arrest in 1998 and was immediately struck that Patricia believed that "the government has had her on their 'list' for many years."[131] Patricia's suspicion that the government has constantly monitored her throughout her lifetime reflected the paranoid feelings in her. Eric, along with his siblings, was brought up in a family culture strewn with conspiracy theories, strict religious interpretations, and contradictions. "She didn't want her kids to have Social Security numbers, but made sure to claim her own benefits and qualify for government-subsidized housing programs."[132] Patricia was skeptical of any government run programs, especially ones touted as beneficial to society.

> The Rudolph's were strict naturopaths. None of the children were vaccinated against childhood disease.[133]

Every action in the Rudolph house seemed to have a religious overtone. Patricia used a strict religious-based discipline approach in the household that was based on the premise that "children are like animals, they have to be trained to learn the commands of their elders…The children are required to memorize biblical proverbs"[134] as a daily routine and as part of their chores. If the children deviated from the routine or did not complete their prescribed chores and biblical memorization, they were punished.

> They would be warned once if there was an infraction. And the second time they would be paddled, pants down.[135]

---

[131] Vollers, *Lone Wolf,* 243.

[132] Henry Schuster and Charles Stone, *Hunting Eric Rudolph: An Insider*'s *Account of the Five-Year Search for the Olympic Bomber* (New York: Berkley Publishing Group, 2005), 166.

[133] Vollers, *Lone Wolf,* 246.

[134] Ibid., 248.

[135] Ibid., 246.

B. EDUCATION, TRAINING, AND THE FOUNDATIONS OF IDEOLOGY

Eric Rudolph did not spend a great deal of time in the public schools. The public schools represented a government conspiracy to Patricia and she felt it was aimed at shaping young minds to conform to a very particular way of thinking. She home schooled Rudolph until the 9th grade. "Pat did not want her family indoctrinated with beliefs which she disapproved of."[136] Rudolph's father, Robert, was diagnosed with cancer when his son was thirteen. He grew very ill and money became tight in the Rudolph household. Tom Branham, a lifelong friend of Robert's and close friend to the family, agreed to help out and take Eric to live with him in Nantahala, North Carolina. This is where the real, hard-core radicalization of Eric Rudolph would begin.

Robert Rudolph died when Eric was fourteen years old. Eric had already been in North Carolina for a few months so the family, having nowhere else to go, moved from Florida to Nantahala, North Carolina so Branham could help them.

> Even though his father was removed from Eric's life early on, there was a father figure. That man was Tom Branham. And according to some reports, he was not a good influence.[137]

This is a stunning understatement. Tom Branham was a radical, religious fringe-dweller who proselytized some of the same radical anti-government and strict religious beliefs as Eric's mother, except multiplied tenfold.

Tom Branham immediately made a significant impression on Eric. Tom was a racist, neo-Nazi, survivalist who espoused anti-government sentiments, and "evolved from Christian fundamentalism into a kind of apocalyptic ultraconservatism."[138] Branham did assist the Rudolph's when they got to North Carolina and quickly became like a member of their family.

---

[136] Walls, *Man Hunt,* 7.

[137] Ibid., 8.

[138] Vollers, *Lone Wolf,* 96.

[He] helped school the younger children in a subsistence style of living. They grew their own vegetables, raised chickens and goats, heated the cabin with firewood they cut from the plentiful forest and piped water into the house from a spring on the property. This was exactly the type of lifestyle that would foster an independent thinker and a rugged survivalist.[139]

Eric was exposed to ample neo-Nazi literature at Branham's house. "Tom had these books about the holocaust. Eric was reading them over there at his house."[140] Branham's radical religious beliefs affected both Eric and his mother. Branham believed "the Aryan race is the true lineage of Israel and Jews are descended from a diabolical union between Satan and Eve."[141] Branham would also have talks with Eric about:

The coming confrontation between the forces of good and evil. He stockpiled supplies, hoarded books, and combed flea markets for anything he might find useful in the coming conflagration.[142]

Branham's influence over a young Eric Rudolph was great, and would be proven effective when Eric entered public school as a ninth grader in Nantahala.

Eric's educational capacities and abilities have not been discussed until this point because before the ninth grade, when he entered public school, there are no records to indicate he had ever been formally tested. Nantahala High School tested him and "his test scores indicated an average intelligence...he had superior language abilities."[143] Tom Branham's influence on Eric bound to the forefront during Eric's freshman year when he "wrote a paper questioning the historical reality of the Nazi German Holocaust."[144] In interviews with his classmates, as the FBI was searching for Eric, one girl stated he was

---

[139] Walls, *Man Hunt,* 9.

[140] Vollers, *Lone Wolf,* 249.

[141] Michael Barkun, *Religion and the Racist Right: The Origins of the Christian Identity Movement,* Rev. ed. (Chapel Hill, NC: University of North Carolina Press, 1997), 173–174.

[142] Vollers, *Lone Wolf,* 96.

[143] Ibid., 101.

[144] Beau Seegmiller, "Radicalized Margins: Eric Rudolph and Religious Violence," *Terrorism and Political Violence*, Volume 19, Number 4 (2007): 523.

always "mouthing off about queers, dykes, and niggers."[145] Eric did not socialize with his classmates and he was viewed as a loner who had few friends; however, he did meet his first girlfriend at Nantahala High School. She described his as:

> Shy to the point of paranoia. He didn't want his picture taken, saying it could be used against him…Sometimes he would leave school on a Friday afternoon and spend the weekend alone in the woods, returning to school on Monday morning in the same, dirty clothes.[146]

Needless to say, it did not work out with the girlfriend. This would become a common theme throughout Eric's life. He was handsome enough and easily attracted women; however, he could never make an emotional connection to maintain a relationship of any sort. Eric only lasted in the public school until the tenth grade before dropping out and returning to the isolation of home schooling.

Tom Branham was just the beginning of the myriad of bad influences Eric would encounter during his teenage years. Branham got "arrested and charged with possession of three unregistered firearms."[147] Nord Davis represented Branham in court and, because of this connection, Davis became the next wily influence in Eric Rudolph's impressionable life. Eventually, the firearm charge was dropped, but a connection between Nord Davis and the Rudolph family remained. Davis, an extremist within the Christian Identity sect, believed "that Caucasians were the true lost tribe of Israel, and that the Bible was the history of the white race, not the story of the Jews."[148] As the Rudolph family became acquainted with Nord Davis over the course of Branham's legal battle, Davis recommended they travel to his church in Missouri to be trained within the Church of Israel. This trip facilitated another curious influence on Eric Rudolph's teen years: Dan Gayman, the founder of the Missouri based Church of Israel.

---

[145] Vollers, *Lone Wolf,* 101.

[146] Ibid., 102.

[147] Schuster and Stone, *Hunting Eric Rudolph*, 182.

[148] Ibid.

Patricia Rudolph took Branham's advice and drove Eric and his brother to Schell City, Missouri to see Dan Gayman when Eric was 18. "Pat describes the family's brush with the Identity sect as just another attempt at chasing the religious rainbow."[149] Eric would spend an entire winter at the compound. When questioned by the FBI about Eric's winter at the Identity compound, two fellow Christian Identity followers that had been there at the time stated:

> Eric was definitely a believer of Christian Identity, even before he got to Schell City. They said he had been influenced in that direction by his neighbor …who they described as a violent man.[150]

That, of course, was Tom Branham.

Eric adopted many of the extreme Christian Identity worldviews; one of those views was on anti-abortion. This was the prodigious issue for Eric Rudolph growing up with a mother who was an anti-abortionist, and would be further emphasized through the Christian Identity church. The Christian Identity belief was that abortion was gravely wrong when it involved members of the chosen race, the white race.

> Eric's calculus about abortion was based more on race than anything else. He felt that if white women continued to get abortions, then pretty soon demographics would take over, and the white race would find itself in the minority.[151]

Eric found some temporary female companionship at the compound, where he dated two Identity Sect girls. One of the girls was Dan Gayman's daughter. Eric felt as if Gayman was trying to control him so he rejected him. When Eric was not willing to wholly "conform to the group's doctrine"[152] the relationships with the girls did not work out, either. The full extent of the influence that winter at the Church of Israel had on Eric Rudolph is unknown.

---

[149] Vollers, *Lone Wolf,* 250.

[150] Schuster and Stone, *Hunting Eric Rudolph*, 187.

[151] Ibid., 193–194.

[152] Maryanne Vollers, *Lone Wolf,* 105.

His sister-in-law, Deborah, stated that he frequently made statements referring to Jews and blacks derogatorily. She claimed he frequently called the television the electronic Jew...he referred to gay people as faggots or Sodomites.[153]

His sister believed many of these views had been intensified at the Christian Identity compound. After returning from the compound in 1985, Rudolph applied for college. He began taking classes at Western Carolina University but he did not last long. "Eric spent two semesters at WCU, taking mostly history and art."[154] Rudolph, again, struggled to fit in, could not make friends, and was not accepted as a member of the group. "Eric had trouble getting along with his fellow students and his professors, who described him as haughty and argumentative in class."[155] He dropped out of college and retreated back to familiar surroundings: living with his mother at home.

Rudolph was exposed to a myriad of influences from the time he moved in with Tom Branham to the time he dropped out of college.

> So this was the education of Eric Rudolph, a syllabus of hate, partly self-guided and partly influenced by his mother, Tom Branham, Dan Gayman, Nord Davis, and the Church of Israel. Many of the virulent strains that were part of the extremist Right—from Christian Identity to the Freedom Movement – went into his intellectual makeup and helped him shape his worldview.[156]

Rudolph had failed to fit in with any group in his life. He was mostly isolated most from public school, and therefore social interaction, by his mom. When he did get to attend school he did not fit in and was a loner. His mother took him on a religious journey that would end for him where it began, lost. His quest for a faith family only harbored in him more confusion. He made no emotional attachments to women other than his mother. He thirsted for something else in his life. Eric Rudolph enlisted in the Army at age 20.

---

[153] Walls, *Man Hunt*, 25.

[154] Maryanne Vollers, *Lone Wolf*, 106.

[155] Ibid.

[156] Schuster and Stone, *Hunting Eric Rudolph*, 191.

C.   LIFE IN THE MILITARY

Eric Rudolph's military career was a brief one. He joined because "he wanted to be part of an elite military unit, like the Rangers or the Special Forces."[157] Eric was searching for a venue where he could succeed and be accepted as part of the group, one of the guys. Rudolph became an Infantryman, trained in basic Infantry skills such as rifle marksmanship, small unit tactics, survival skills, and weapon affects. This would serve as an important ingredient to Rudolph's terrorist campaign in the coming years, equipping him with the appropriate mental capital to construct explosives and survive in the woods of Nantahala, effectively evading the FBI during their five-year man hunt to find him. The few Army buddies he had, stated that he:

> Railed about how the government had too much power and how he hated paying taxes He loved everything that was German; his bunkmates remembered him openly praising Adolf Hitler. He ranted about Jews and the banks and the media.[158]

The culture of the Army did not suit Rudolph's racist sensibilities. Rudolph's mother recalls "Eric's problem with the Army was black drill sergeants."[159] After becoming completely disenfranchised with his military experience, he came up with a plan to get kicked out of the Army by taking drugs and purposely failing an Army drug test. All in all, Rudolph spent only 18 months in the Army, getting out when he was only twenty-two. He was discharged after intentionally failing multiple drug tests.

D.   LOCAL CRIMINAL TO TERRORIST

Eric Rudolph had failed, again, to find a group where he belonged. He simply could not bring himself to conform to the military. After his short stint in the Army, he returned back to the Nantahala area. Rudolph would begin to isolate himself in the

---

[157] Vollers, *Lone Wolf,* 106.

[158] Ibid., 107.

[159] Schuster and Stone, *Hunting Eric Rudolph,* 192.

forests of Nantahala. "Rudolph was truly dependent on no one, and trusted nobody. It was a habit of solitude he developed early in his life."[160]

> [He] learned to hunt and fish, studied herbal medicine, and fashioned himself as an Army survivalist. For cash, he became a backwoods pot farmer and enjoyed the fruits of his work, getting stoned, and watching Cheech & Chong movies.[161]

He attempted to recruit a couple of his Army buddies to come out to North Carolina and join him in his marijuana business but they all rejected him. Rudolph was paranoid that the government was on his trail and was always looking over his shoulder. "Rudolph lived by picking up odd jobs…He operated on a cash-only basis and avoided the use of his social security number."[162]

Rudolph had limited connection with society at this point. He dated a few women, but every relationship ended badly for him. His mother remained the only personal connection in his life at this point. Rudolph would spend the next few years concentrating on his marijuana business. A neighbor who moved into the area and met Rudolph found it odd that "at twenty-nine years old he was still living with his mother."[163]

As Eric Rudolph radicalized in the isolation of the Nantahala forest, his ideology took shape. He began to take his anger out on the local community by committing petty crimes. Even Tom Branham noticed Eric Rudolph was different after returning from the Army. "He noticed that Rudolph had returned from the army a different person, more radical, bitter, and secretive."[164] Tom Branham and Eric Rudolph stopped speaking around the end of 1995.

---

[160] Vollers, *Lone Wolf,* 100.

[161] Paul Cuadros et al., "How luck ran out for a most wanted fugitive," *Time,* June 9, 2003, 8.

[162] Seegmiller, "Radicalized Margins: Eric Rudolph and Religious Violence", 524.

[163] Vollers, *Lone Wolf,* 112.

[164] Ibid., 111.

Branham claimed Eric shot his daughter's pet cat. When Branham confronted him, Rudolph said the cat was killing wild rabbits that he might need to hunt to survive someday.[165]

Rudolph became a voracious reader at this time. He bought Tim McVeigh's book, *All American Monster*, and felt he understood his plight. Rudolph's friend asked him, "'Do you think Tim McVeigh is an American Hero?' 'He would be to a lot of people' Eric replied. "[166] Eric confided to the same friend that "the Olympics would be the next target for terrorists to make a statement."[167] It was around this time, in 1996, when Rudolph took the next step in his pattern of radicalization after being out of the Army for seven years, working odd jobs, and tending to his marijuana business. Rudolph sold his family home in May of 1996 and began a secretive life not even his mother knew about. Eric ranted about the "New World Order and the Jews."[168] He was convinced the world would erupt in a war at any moment. Interestingly enough, his concern for the 'New World Order' was exactly the plight of Timothy McVeigh that he had just read in McVeigh's biography. Rudolph took the money he made off the family home, told his family he was headed west, and bought himself a trailer using an alias. He "rented a trailer under the name Bob Randolph."[169] Eric trusted no one. He slipped from society altogether.

E.   ERIC RUDOLPH THE TERRORIST

Eric Rudolph had set the conditions to begin his terror campaign. He had hard cash from the sale of his family home, he paid for everything in cash, he rented a trailer under an alias, and no one knew where he was. Rudolph found himself a trailer in the town of Murphy, within the Nantahala area, further secluded within the forest. Rudolph began to plan his first bombing, the Olympic park bombing in Atlanta during the 1996 Summer Olympic games.

---

[165] Vollers, *Lone Wolf,* 112.

[166] Schuster and Stone, *Hunting Eric Rudolph*, 195.

[167] Ibid., 196.

[168] Walls, *Man Hunt,* 35.

[169] Vollers, *Lone Wolf,* 113.

Eric Rudolph lived like a specter in and around Murphy for the next year and a half. He paid cash to rent places for a few months at a time, then moved on.[170]

Rudolph prepared a pipe bomb for the Olympic games and delivered it on July 27, 1996.

> A week into the Olympics, 50,000 people were gathered in Centennial Olympic Park to hear a band called Jack Mack and the Heart Attack. It was in that crowd, at 1:27 a.m., that a pipe bomb exploded, spattering blood across the new plaza.[171]

Rudolph's bomb killed two and wounded over 100 in the attack. Rudolph explained the rationale behind his attack.

> Under the protection and auspices of the regime in Washington, millions of people came out to celebrate the ideals of global socialism…Even though the purpose of the Olympics is to promote these despicable ideals, the purpose of the attack on July 27 was to confound, anger, and embarrass the Washington government in the eyes of the world for its abominable sanctioning of abortion on demand.[172]

Rudolph's selection of his first target was a strategic one that would promote his agenda to millions.

Rudolph struck again on January 16, 1997 at an abortion clinic in Sandy Springs, Georgia, that injured five. Rudolph set up two bombs in this case. He fashioned one bomb to detonate against his primary target, the clinic, and the second bomb targeted the first responders. "The bomber had clearly set a trap, placing a secondary device exactly where he knew law enforcement officers and first responders would gather."[173] This is a case of classic Army infantry tactics here. I know because I have received the same training. Rudolph bombed a lesbian bar in Atlanta on February 21, 1997 that injured five people. He stated at his trial in 2005 that "he targeted the Otherside Lounge in

---

[170] Vollers, *Lone Wolf,* 114.

[171] Ellen Barry, "The Nation; Atlanta Olympics Bomber Apologizes to His Victims; Eric Rudolph, given four consecutive life terms, says he accepts responsibility," *The Los Angeles Times,* August 23, 2005, 10.

[172] Schuster and Stone, *Hunting Eric Rudolph,* 345.

[173] Vollers, *Lone Wolf,* 36.

Atlanta…because he felt that the gay rights movement was a direct assault upon the long-term health and integrity of civilization."[174] After completing the bombings of the clinic and lesbian bar Rudolph sent a message to the media in Atlanta. He stated:

> [The bombings had been] carried out by units of the Army of God…those who participate in <u>any way</u> in the murder of children may be targeted for attack…The attack in midtown was aimed at the sodomite bar (The Otherside). We will target sodomites, their organizations, and all those who push their agenda…The code for out unit is 4-1-9-9-3. Death to the New World Order.[175]

The number sequence Rudolph used in his message sent a clear indication to authorities that they were dealing with someone who fashioned himself part of the greater agenda of the right.

> April 19, 1993 was the day the compound at Waco burned to the ground. Two years later, to the day, Timothy McVeigh blew up the Murrah Federal Building…And Death to the New World Order was a rallying cry for a broad spectrum of anti-government, anti-Semitic fanatics.[176]

The last bombing Rudolph executed before the FBI discovered his identity was a second abortion clinic bombing, this time in Birmingham, Alabama. The bomb killed a security guard and severely wounded a nurse who worked there. Rudolph believed the bombing and subsequent killing of clinic workers was justifiable. When discussing the bombing at his trial in 2005, Rudolph stated, "What they did was participate in the murder and dismemberment of upward of 50 children a week…Abortion is murder, I believe that deadly force is indeed justified in an attempt to stop it."[177] He sent another letter to the media in Atlanta to explain the Birmingham abortion clinic bomb. He stated:

---

[174] Ellen Barry and Jenny Jarvie, "The Nation: Rudolph Admits Bombing '96 Olympic Park; The defiant ex-fugitive cites hatred of abortion, government, sanctions," *Los Angeles Times*, April 14, 2005, 11.

[175] Vollers, *Lone Wolf,* 44–45.

[176] Ibid., 46.

[177] Jay Reeves, "Clinic Bomber Gets 2 Life Sentences; Rudolph is Unrepentant, Says Abortion Must Be Fought With Deadly Force," *The Washington Post*, July 19, 2005, A05.

The bombing in Birmingham was carried out by the Army of God...Let those who work in the murder mill be warned once more—you will be targeted without quarter...your commissars in Washington can't protect you![178]

Rudolph's vehicle was identified as he left the scene after the bombing.

Washington was lucky that day in Birmingham, they had a witness who happened into a fortuitous position, and my truck was identified...I knew something was amiss based on the early reports out of Birmingham, so I prepared to make a move as I debated within myself whether or not to run or to fight them in court. I chose the woods.[179]

Rudolph would disappear into the forests of North Carolina and lead the FBI on a five year manhunt to find him.

F.   AFTERMATH OF BOMBINGS

Eric Rudolph vanished into the forests of North Carolina. A trained survivalist, he purchased groceries the night he went on the run.

The bill was $109.96. Eric paid cash. Later the FBI would calculate the weight of the groceries, put it at seventy-two pounds. And they would bring in nutritionists, who said it was enough to last a man six months.[180]

Eric would defy the odds in evading authorities as they searched the area with over 200 agents. He was nowhere to be found.

Eric Rudolph quickly became a hero to many locals living in the area. This may explain how he survived in the forest for over five years. After months of searching by the FBI and local law enforcement, the FBI thought that locals had to be helping Rudolph.

---

[178] Schuster and Stone, *Hunting Eric Rudolph*, 89.

[179] Barry and Jarvie, "The Nation; Rudolph Admits Bombing '96 Olympic Park.", 1.

[180] Schuster and Stone, *Hunting Eric Rudolph*, 86.

In Rudolph's case the violence seems mitigated by another 'achievement,' namely the outsmarting of government officials and bounty hunters. In this regard, Rudolph is a populist hero, a hillbilly who, like his third-world counterparts, make a mockery of modernity.[181]

The issue was many of the locals not only empathized with Eric, they agreed with what he had done, especially concerning hot button issues like abortion and homosexuality. In many of the local communities, the residents were openly supportive of Rudolph. In the town of Murphy, where Rudolph had lived for a while, "the Peachtree Restaurant, tears welled in the eyes of owner Betty Howard, 47, as she discussed the message on the marquee outside her eatery. It says, Pray for Eric Rudolph."[182] Another local resident stated:

> If he did that Olympic Bombing, he should be punished...But as far as those abortion clinics and the gay club is concerned, he shouldn't be punished for that. You see, those things are not right in the sight of God.[183]

Rudolph did whatever was necessary to evade the authorities. The intense manhunt underway placed enough pressure on Rudolph that he was not able to continue his terror campaign during his five years in the forest. He did conduct petty crimes to support his lifestyle. He would rob grain mills for food, break into homes, or even steal a vehicle if he knew he could get away with it. Eric knew he could talk to no one so he "exercised his voice by talking to himself in his camp, and reading aloud books and newspapers...debate the issues, taking both sides and acting them out in different voices."[184]

The Rudolph family did not take the news of Eric's suspect status well. Eric's mom believed in his innocence. The Rudolph family was under constant surveillance by the FBI in case Eric ever contacted them. The strangest response from the Rudolph

---

[181] Carol Mason, "The Hillbilly Defense: Culturally Mediating U.S. Terror at Home and Abroad," *NWSA Journal* (2005): Vol. 17, 3.

[182] Michael Fletcher, "At Home, Rudolph Wins Sympathy; Distrust of Government Widespread in Area," *The Washington Post,* June 4, 2003, A2.

[183] Ibid., A2.

[184] Vollers, *Lone Wolf,* 184.

family came from Eric's brother, Daniel. He did not believe Eric was guilty of any crimes and after multiple, redundant interviews with the FBI, Daniel snapped. He decided to make a video for the media in support of his brother's innocence.

> On Sunday, March 8, 1998, he used a particularly grizzly and attention-getting means to quietly protest what he saw as the FBI's persecution of his brother…He tied a tourniquet around his left arm, set up a video camera facing his table saw in the garage, turned it on and then proceeded to cut off his own hand at the wrist.[185]

Eric Rudolph made a fatal error that led to his arrest on May 31, 2003. Rudolph decided to leave the safety of the forest and come into the town of Murphy in the middle of the night to rummage for supplies.

> In the early morning hours, rookie cop Jeff Postell spotted a thin man in an alley behind the Save-A-Lot Food store in Murphy…He was very cooperative, not a bit disrespectful, says Postell, 21, who arrested him. Another officer called to the scene recognized Rudolph.[186]

G. IDEOLOGY OF ERIC RUDOLPH

A lot has been revealed about the ideology of Eric Rudolph since his capture and it begins with his manifesto. "The piece from his writings that provides us with the most insight is his own 'Manifesto' of sorts, which he distributed in handwritten form after entering his guilty pleas in court on April 13, 2005.[187] Rudolph carried out his attacks with a good deal of thought as to their tactical and strategic consequences. He wanted to get his message out to the world. His "larger strategic objective: the displacement of centrally visible features of American society such as legalized abortions, the open acceptance of homosexuality, and the global transnational economic system that countenances and supports such social degradations."[188] Rudolph believed abortion was murder and there was no debate. He stated, "when the regime in Washington legalized,

---

[185] Walls, *Man Hunt,* 26–27.

[186] Paul Cuadros et al., "How luck ran out for a most wanted fugitive," 8.

[187] Seegmiller, "Radicalized Margins," 516.

[188] Ibid.

sanctioned and legitimized this practice, they forfeited their legitimacy and moral authority to govern."[189] Further, because Washington sanctioned such action, Rudolph felt entitled to strike back.

Rudolph's worldview was closest to that of a Christian Identity believer postulating an anti-abortionist, anti-homosexual, racist agenda. He believed the government was watching and would strike at any moment. He felt justified to take the fight to the government in the name of what he believed. "He was concerned about the permissiveness of secular authorities in the United States and 'the atheistic internationalism' controlling one side of the culture war in modern society."[190] Rudolph viewed himself as a cultural warrior on a legitimate side of a battle he deemed relevant and central to his existence. Rudolph's doctrine, in the end, was truly all he had because the more he lost along the road that was his life, the more fiercely he clung to what little remained.

H.   ANALYSIS OF ERIC RUDOLPH

It would be hard to orchestrate a more dastardly lineup of misfits to act as Eric Rudolph's earliest influences and inspirations than the ones who actively served in that role. This crew starts with his mother Patricia Rudolph. "Rudolph was extremely close to his mother and adopted many of her religious beliefs."[191] She instilled in Eric an intransigent, rigid suspicion and mistrust of the government, a confusing religious voyage that led him to the religious fringe of Christian Identity and the Church of Israel, and led him to the damaging mentorship of racist, anti-government, religious, conspiracy theorists like Tom Branham, Dan Gayman, and Nord Davis.

Eric Rudolph's mother isolated him from society from the very start. She kept him out of public school and safe from what she interpreted as a dangerous curriculum concealing a government conspiracy. On the few occasions that Eric did attend public

---

[189] Barry and Jarvie, "The Nation,"1.

[190] Mark Juergensmeyer, *Terror in the Mind of God: The Global Rise of Religious Violence* (Berkeley, CA: University of California Press, 2003), 31.

[191] Terrie Turchie and Kathleen Pucket, *Hunting The American Terrorist: The FBI's War on Homegrown Terror* (New York: History Publishing Company, LLC, 2007), 264.

school, he was an outcast, a loner, and could never escape the isolationism that he had been conditioned to accept. Eric dated a few girls in his life, even achieved physical relationships with a few; however, it is important to emphasize that the relationship with his mother served as his only lasting personal relationship with a woman.

Rudolph fashioned himself a survivalist. He had stockpiled and buried weapons in the woods behind his house to be ready when the Federal Government came. He always felt government agents would materialize at any moment. He increasingly isolated himself as he devolved into his radicalized viewpoint and, of course, he sequestered himself in the Nantahala forest once he became aware of the FBI's manhunt for him.

Rudolph was convinced his ideology was religiously valid and, therefore, correct in the eyes of God, regardless of what the law stated. The Federal Government's sanctioning of abortion and acceptance of homosexuality delegitimized their authority and sanctioned him to act. The issues of abortion, homosexuality, and the infringing U.S. government on citizen's rights permitted Rudolph to retaliate. In his Manifesto he stated: "there is no more legitimate reason to my knowledge, for renouncing allegiance to and if necessary using force to bring down this monstrosity of a government to the dust where it belongs."[192]

Rudolph had never been successful attaining membership or feeling like he was part of a group. He failed to fit in his schools, dropped out of college, failed to find the right religious identity, could not make it in the Army, could not convince his former Army buddies to come out to North Carolina and join him in his Marijuana business, could not maintain female companionship, and once he began his violence, was not accepted by the peaceful anti-abortion movement in the country. The single thing that did not reject Eric Rudolph in his life, was his ideology. He gave his heart and soul to his ideology knowing it was the one thing that no one could take away from him.

---

[192] Vollers, *Lone Wolf,* 288.

Eric Rudolph now resides at the Supermax prison, along with Ted Kaczynski, in Florence, Colorado. Like his contemporaries, has never wavered from his rigid ideological beliefs to this day. From his cell of isolation, he communicates with the American public through the Web site *Army of God*. He has published an enormous amount of literature to date, shared on the Web site, and has become an icon of sorts to the extreme right anti-abortionist culture.

THIS PAGE INTENTIONALLY LEFT BLANK

V.   THE LONE WOLF DOMESTIC TERRORIST EXPOSED

The parallels that exist within the pattern of radicalization between Tim McVeigh, Ted Kaczynski, and Eric Rudolph are striking. As I began my research into each of the three lone wolf terrorists I thought there would be similarities; however, I was unprepared for my analysis to reveal identical characteristics on so many levels. The final analysis of this data is a delicate balance. After analyzing each terrorist, it was quickly established they shared many things in common; however, random, individual commonality proves nothing.

> [It would be extremely] difficult to identify predictors of potential terrorists from this picture. Very many people share the kinds of attributes that can be identified. The reasons for this may be that there are, perhaps, no special causes of terrorism, in the sense of a common class of explanations…Rather a complex set of circumstances, dependent upon the chance occurrence of events within facilitating contexts, represents the individual's causal story; each individual, perhaps, having a different and unique one.[193]

The distinction comes when the individual terrorist's pattern of radicalization is shown to occur on the same chronological timeline as that of his contemporaries. It is this common chronological pattern, comprised of the ideological beliefs, psychological factors, attributes, traits, training, and education common to my three case studies that reveal the warning signs and markers of potential lone wolf domestic terrorists.

A.   CHRONOLOGICAL PATTERNS OF RADICALIZATION EMERGE

The childhood, family life, and home environments of McVeigh, Kazcynski, and Rudolph were damaging for each of them. Tim McVeigh's parents were not around often and placed their careers ahead of raising their lower-middle class family. His father worked long hours, while McVeigh's mother was gone days at a time tending to her job as a flight attendant. Tim spent a lot of his time fending for himself; conditioned to be a loner. When his parents got divorced, he blamed his mother; angry that she would not

---

[193] Maxwell Taylor, *The Terrorist* (London: Brassey's Defence Publishers, 1988), 139.

71

accept the traditional stay-at-home mother role. She had not taken care of him. Ted Kaczynski's parents, also lower middle-class, placed academic achievement over all else in the their household. The academic pressure on Ted was intense; they forced him to skip two grades, ultimately leading him to become an outcast and the brunt of ridicule by his classmates. His parents' academic vehemence caused him to slip into isolation and become a consummate loner. Eric Rudolph's mother was borderline radical in her beliefs. She exposed Eric to the radical right and a host of nefarious influences. She homeschooled him, indoctrinating him into her rigid, religiously flavored worldview. She conditioned Eric to accept that life was very private. He would accept his private, isolated lifestyle as normal. The few times he did get to go to public school he was out of his element and was treated as an outcast. Although McVeigh, Kazcynski, and Rudolph's childhood stories are different, they all were led to the same place, a life where isolation and loneliness and significant pressure from within the family to be, to perform, to be anyone but oneself, was not out of the ordinary.

The isolationism cultivated during childhood for McVeigh, Kaczynski, and Rudolph led to three common trends that chronologically emerged for each of them during their radicalization process. Isolation contributed heavily to the formation of their individual ideologies. Each trend is uniquely related to the other. First, all three terrorists displayed the desire to be a member of a group but found in the end they had difficulty being accepted, feeling a part of, or succeeding in a group. Second, each terrorist would struggle to make an intimate emotional connection with another human being. This was highlighted by their inability to attain female companionship. Third, the isolationism, lack of group acceptance or success within a group, and difficulty establishing emotional connections led to each of them viewing themselves as the ultimate loners: survivalists.

The desire to be part of a group was common between McVeigh, Kaczynski, and Rudolph, and contributed to their radicalization process. Tim McVeigh and Eric Rudolph both entered college only to find out they did not fit in, and dropped out after a only a couple of semesters. After dropping out of school, they both joined the Army and had aspiration of becoming elite Soldiers in the Special Forces or Rangers; however, found they were not tough enough, could not conform to Army life, and failed. Ted Kaczynski was told his whole life that he was an academic, he was brilliant, and he had great potential to make contributions to the academic venue. He graduated from Harvard and Michigan and took a job as a professor at Berkeley only to find hate welling in him against the very academic lifestyle he had tried so hard to embody. His profession stood for everything that was wrong with society, especially the focus on technology and industrialization. He quit his job and moved to the forest, where he could think more clearly.

After finding they failed to fit into a group, or could not succeed or feel comfortable when they were in a group, each man attempted to create his own. Tim McVeigh rallied his former Army buddies, Michael Fortier and Terry Nichols, to help him with his plot against the Government. He spoke of the inevitable 'New World Order' the U.S. government would soon impose on the unsuspecting American population. McVeigh had aspirations of inciting the same grand revolution that his hero Earl Turner had in his fictional book, *The Turner Diaries*. *The Turner Diaries* started a revolution the country by attacking the FBI headquarters. McVeigh dreamed of attacking something even larger by striking the U.S. government in a grandiose fashion. He struck the Murrah Federal Building on the two-year anniversary of the Waco Siege in an attempt to rally the militia culture of the United States to follow his lead and take action against the New World Order. He believed he would be remembered as a famous American Patriot.

Eric Rudolph tried to recruit a couple of his old Army buddies to join him in the forests of Nantahala, North Carolina but they all rejected him. Once he began his bombings, Rudolph sent letters to the media claiming responsibility for the terrorist acts on behalf of the 'Army of God'. Rudolph would also end each letter with a code to identify his unit, 4-1-9-9-3, and the phrase 'Death to the New World Order'. This message, like McVeigh's, symbolized a cry to the militia culture of the United States to take action. His code was the date of the U.S. government siege on the Waco compound while the phrase 'Death to the New World Order' had already been made famous by

McVeigh. Rudolph, like McVeigh, believed citizens would follow his lead. He would finally be a member of a group, the leader of the Army of God.

Ted Kaczynski hated himself for becoming a mathematician, one of the contributors to the technological and societal advancement he despised that enriched the 'system' created in the United States. Kaczynski, like his contemporaries, could not find his place in a group so he erected his own. As Ted began to bomb airline and university targets, he would send letters to the media and authorities claiming responsibility for the attacks by the group 'Freedom Club'. Kaczynski would place the initials 'FC' in each of his bombs. When he wrote the New York Times and Washington Post to publish his manifesto, he sent it from the 'Freedom Club'. Kaczynski's aim was to make his audience believe they were dealing with a larger movement in the United States that shared the same belief.

McVeigh, Kaczynski, and Rudolph struggled their whole lives to attain female companionship. This is a direct result of how they each were conditioned during their youth to be loners and isolationists. "Their social isolation was linked to and compounded by a lack of satisfactory relationships with women. Kaczynski and, apparently, McVeigh had no physical relationships with women at all."[194] Tim McVeigh lacked the social skills needed to talk to women, which made him come off awkward and inappropriate. His Army buddies made fun of him and thought he was strange for not trying harder. Constantly rejected, he gave up the pursuit of women. Kaczynski nearly lost his mind over not having a woman in his life, contemplating a sex change operation so he could finally touch a woman, by touching himself. The most successful of the three was Eric Rudolph. Eric had no problem establishing the initial connection with a female; however, he never progressed past a purely physical relationship with any of them. Eric's only meaningful relationship was with his mother. Their religious beliefs tied them together although; however, Eric had no problem cutting his mom off after he returned home from the Army. Although their lacking social skills had developed in different ways, those skills would hamstring them from making a personal intimate

---

[194] Turchie and Puckett, *Hunting the American Terrorist*, 265.

relationship. There would be no one to come home to, no one to disappoint, no one to look forward to. Ultimately, there was no one to live for, and that is an important constant condition that existed in each of their lives.

McVeigh, Rudolph, and Kaczynski all fashioned themselves as survivalists. McVeigh told his friends, at age 14, that he was a survivalist. He told them they needed to be prepared for the day the country erupted into violence. He remained a survivalist throughout his lifetime. He rented a storage shed while in the Army to stockpile supplies so he could be ready. He traveled the country following gun shows. He thought the day New World Order would strike was imminent. Ted Kaczynski changed his life from the campus of U.C. Berkeley to the forests of Montana within a month. He would become a consummate survivalist living in the forest for 18 years on a very limited income while he planned and subsequently conducted his terrorist campaign. Eric Rudolph subscribed to the same survivalist dogmas as McVeigh. Paranoid that the New World Order was preparing its strike after the Brady Bill passed in 1994, Eric buried guns and supplies in the forest behind their house. Rudolph would disappear into the forest after becoming a suspect in his bombings as the FBI conducted their large, unsuccessful manhunt for him for five years.

When terrorists like McVeigh, Kaczynski, and Rudolph find themselves alone, not accepted into a group, and isolated, they formulate rigid ideologies to compensate.

> After multiple failures to achieve social connection and acceptance in a group, there's one aspect of the group that is still available to the Lone Wolf: its ideology…he makes the attachment he craves not to a group, but to the ideology itself.[195]

McVeigh, Kaczynski, and Rudolph gave their every being to their ideology. McVeigh was willing to kill hundreds to free the naïve American public from the threatening New World Order. Kaczynski would kill and wound over a hundred people after declaring war on those aiding, improving, and advancing the industrialization and technological advancement of society. Rudolph would kill and injure over a hundred people after declaring the government lost its legitimacy and moral authority to govern after

---

[195] Turchie and Puckett, *Hunting the American Terrorist*, 270.

legalizing abortion and open homosexuality. The lone wolf terrorist feels he has the moral authority to counter attack the morally corrupt force in contradiction with his ideology, regardless of the collateral damage inflicted on innocent bystanders as long as the greater good associated with the individual's ideology is achieved. "The isolation he has felt all his life is replaced by a sense of strong belonging to the cause, the ideology itself, and he can focus all his energy and attention on action in its service."[196]

This leads to the next important point in analyzing this common pattern of radicalization. Each individual's ideology discussed above is not instantly created. Each one of them took years to cultivate their ideologies, until those ideologies finally demanded action. I identified a common turning point in each of McVeigh, Kaczynski, and Rudolph's lives when their ideologies turned from a series of thoughts or beliefs expressed sufficiently through dialogue to something that demanded much more. Tim McVeigh's ideological turning point and serious radicalization began when he left the military in winter of 1991. He went back home in hopes of attaining a good job but found nothing had changed. Everything he believed about the New World Order was seemingly coming true. The Federal Government was proving it through action with Rudy Ridge in 1992, Waco in 1993, and the passing of the Brady Bill in 1994. Just over four years after he was discharged from the military, Tim McVeigh would execute his attack on April 19, 1995.

Ted Kaczynski's ideological turning point and serious radicalization began the day he withdrew from academia, in the summer of 1969. He would search for a remote piece of land sufficient to isolate him from society. He found adequate isolation in the forests of Montana. He would spend months without human contact. He warred against intruders in the local area, and began feverishly writing his journal and manifesto, and developing his plan to get even with society and teach everyone a lesson. It would take just over nine years for Kaczynski to initiate his first attack on May 25, 1978 when he sent a mail bomb to a scientist at Northwestern University. He would continue his attacks for eight additional years finally being captured in April 1996.

---

[196] Turchie and Puckett, *Hunting the American Terrorist*, 271.

Eric Rudolph's ideological turning point, like McVeigh, came after being discharged from the military in the spring of 1988. Rudolph would return home to the forest of North Carolina, benefit from the sale of his family home, and start a secretive life that was unknown even to his family. He grew marijuana, paid for everything in cash, only stayed in one place for a few months before moving on, and constantly remained paranoid of imminent government action by the New World Order. It would take Rudolph just over eight years to carry out his first bombing against Atlanta's Olympic Centennial Park on July 27, 1996. He would carry out three additional bombings, until finally being identified after the Birmingham abortion clinic bombing in January 1998. Rudolph disappeared into the forest of Nantahala for the next five years, and was ultimately captured on May 31, 2003.

Finally, each of these three domestic lone wolf terrorists longed for their voices to be heard and each man was greatly concerned for his own safety. They wanted their messages out, they wanted the American people to sympathize with their plight, join it, take action, and fall into line. Each believed he was individually valuable, crucial to the successful outcome and positive change in line with his ideology. Prior to his bombing, Tim McVeigh wrote letters to local newspapers and travelled to Waco to help the Branch Davidians. The day of the bombing, McVeigh parked his Ryder truck outside the Murrah Federal Building on a five-minute fuse, which was plenty of time for him to escape injury. After the bombing, he was extremely concerned with how he would be remembered. He wanted to get his biography, *American Terrorist,* published before his death so he could tell his story. He believed until the day he died that, eventually, the citizens of this country would realize he was right, he was a patriot, and he did what no one else would do for the benefit of the country.

Ted Kaczynski wrote thousands of pages of text during his eighteen years in the forest of Montana. He wanted the American people to understand why he was bombing so he relayed messages to the authorities and public alike during his bombing campaign. He believed the American people would sympathize with the Freedom Club, join the cause, and fight for the industrialization and technological advancements destroying our country to stop. He built bombs that would kill and maim innocent civilians while never

77

placing himself in a position to be injured. He contacted the *New York Times* and the *Washington Post*, forcing them to publish his manifesto or, he threatened, he would amplify his bombing campaign. Millions read his manifesto. After he was captured and sentenced to life in prison, Rudolph continued his writings. He writes new material to this day and has never waivered on his belief or changed his rigid ideology.

Eric Rudolph never placed himself at risk during any of his bombings, either. He used a timed fuse or command detonated bombs in each of his strikes to ensure his safety. He thought himself too important to the anti-abortionist agenda to be killed. He targeted the American public through his propaganda delivered to media outlets after his bombings. Rudolph's 'Army of God' would send the message loud and clear to the American Public. The Army of God did not tolerate abortion and believed homosexuality should be made illegal by the government. He believed large swaths of the American public would hear the call and join the cause, forcing the Federal Government to reconsider its policies. After his capture, he was very concerned with his legacy and how he would be perceived. Like Kaczynski, he was sentenced to life in prison. He has become an icon to the extreme right anti-abortionist movement and has published numerous articles to date through his website, the Army of God. Like McVeigh and Kaczynski, Rudolph's ideology and beliefs have not waivered.

B. CONCLUSION: LONE WOLF PATTERNS OF RADICALIZATION

Tim McVeigh, Ted Kaczynski, and Eric Rudolph's lives followed similar paths as they journeyed toward a vocation of domestic lone wolf terrorism. Their individual stories are different; however, a common set of circumstances and events unfolded along an analogous chronological path. The conditions surrounding their childhood and adolescent years yielded loners and isolationists. They spent a lot of time by themselves and as a result did not acquire adequate social skills necessary to establish close human relationships. They could not find female companionship, which abated their reasons to stay peaceful and lead normal lives. They yearned to be a member of a group, failed in each attempt, but never stopped trying to attain group status.

McVeigh, Kaczynski, and Rudolph designated themselves survivalists. When they found they did not fit into any groups, they adopted the one thing they had left that no one could take away from them, their ideologies. They poured their hearts and souls into their ideologies. Nothing else mattered to them. An ideology could not reject or abandon them. They all had definable turning points in their lives during which it became no longer acceptable to explain their ideologies through discussion. They isolated themselves, cut off contact with their families and began to stew. Once in isolation, their ideologies would take shape and slowly inch them closer to the line of direct action, violence in the name of their ideologies. From that definable turning point, it would take McVeigh over four years, Kaczynski nine years, and Rudolph eight years to strike.

McVeigh, Kaczynski, and Rudolph believed they were important. They would be the men to take the blinders off the bourgeois American citizens. They would ensure their individual safety and not risk injury like they would to their innocent but expendable victims. They would deliver their agenda's to the American people, through the media after violence, manifestos, and personal biographies. In the end, none would accomplish his objectives. The American public would not join their cause or adopt their rigid ideologies.

Each domestic lone wolf terrorist would eventually fall into oblivion, his story largely forgotten. Timothy McVeigh would be executed while Ted Kaczynski and Eric Rudolph would spend the rest of their lives sharing a lonely hallway in isolation in prison. In the end, their only legacy would be found in providing suitable case studies to help answer the question of what makes individuals radicalize into domestic lone wolf terrorists. The next lone wolf domestic terrorist lurks in our midst, and could be following the same chronological pattern that we saw with McVeigh, Kaczynski, and Rudolph. Apply the chronological pattern of radicalization demonstrated to us by the three most prolific lone wolf domestic terrorists this country has ever seen to future radicalization and we could catch it upstream, before it happens.

Home-Grown Violent Extremist and Recognizing Indicators of Radicalization

While prosecuting the war on terrorism abroad, along with the implementation of enhanced security measures, we've been fairly successful in deterring attacks in the United States. To counter our efforts, Al-Qaeda and other terrorist organizations have adapted their tactics for recruiting and radicalizing individuals in order to carry out attacks on us and our allies. While it's still possible to recruit individuals, organize them into cells, and conduct organized attacks using their usual methodology, centrally controlled or dictated attacks are the exception and not the rule. In our country, the attacks are less sophisticated and carried out by radicalized individuals typically described as "lone wolves" or as we say in Army-speak, "Homegrown Violent Extremists (HVE). From 2001 to 2009, there were 91 HVE attacks against the US. The recruitment of lone wolf terrorists is especially insidious since recruited individuals don't fit the typical "terrorist mold" with most being U.S. citizens without any criminal record, without long-term exposure to radical Islamic influences, having adequate or above-average educations, and working decent jobs.

While we can statistically categorize people who are typically susceptible or at high risk for terrorist recruitment and radicalization, surveilling this segment of the population would not be legal or practical; therefore, we must understand the process of the recruitment and radicalization of lone wolf terrorists and recognize the indicators of radicalization so that we can foil their plots and incarcerate them.

Most experts describe the Radicalization Process in four distinct stages:

- ☐ Stage 1: Pre-Radicalization
- ☐ Stage 2: Self-Identification
- ☐ Stage 3: Indoctrination
- ☐ Stage 4: Jihadization

In the first stage, Pre-Radicalization, individuals typically lead "ordinary" lives. As stated before, they come from nearly all walks of life (professional, blue-collar, white-collar, military, etc.), typically having no criminal history and working ordinary jobs. Then, something tragic occurs in their rather "uneventful lives" where these individuals are alienated or disassociated from the rest of society. This event could be losing a job, losing an investment, a divorce, a tragic accident, or a death in the family. Sometimes, these types of events affect our soldiers also placing them at risk for recruitment. When this occurs, these individuals search for spiritual guidance and give them cause to seek meaning to their existence, or, perhaps, find group membership to fill gaps left by a broken or failing family (Stage 2, Self-Identification). While there are a number of paths for these individuals to realize their new identity (such as schools, mosques where radical Imams preach, or in prisons), most often, they turn to the most convenient, non-intimidating path providing a sense of anonymity and security, the Internet. Self-radicalization begins the day that an individual seeks out jihadist websites. Continued online association or correspondence may point him/her to other resources like other local jihadist mentors and likeminded fanatics furthering his/her Indoctrination (Stage 3). When the individual has been sufficiently indoctrinated and convinced to take action to support the cause of Radical Islamic Jihad, he/she has entered the final and most dangerous stage of the Radicalization Process. It is at this stage, when we depend on our ability to recognize the Indicator of Radicalization.

Over the years, experts have determined behavior patterns common to HVEs. These behavior patterns are the following:

1. Advocating violence, the threat of violence, or use of force to achieve goals that are political, religious, or ideological in nature.

2. Advocating support for international terrorist organizations or objectives.

3. Providing financial or other material support to a terrorist organization or to someone suspected of being a terrorist.

4. Association with or connections to known or suspected terrorists.

5. Repeated expression of hatred and intolerance of American society, culture, government, or principles of the U.S. Constitution.

6. Repeated visiting or browsing of Internet websites that promote of advocate violence directed against the United States of U.S. forces, or that promote International Terrorism or terrorist themes without official sanction in the performance of duties.

7. Expressing an obligation to engage in violence in support of International Terrorism or inciting others to do the same.

8. Purchasing bomb making materials or obtaining information about the construction of explosives.

9. Active attempts to encourage others to violate laws, disobey lawful orders or regulations, or disrupt military activities.

10. Family ties to known or suspected international terrorist or terrorist supporters.

Although there are many of us who might have reservations on reporting individuals exhibiting these behaviors because we might be labeled as racists, bigots, or not supporting Army Equal Employment Opportunity (EEO), it must be understood, that if these behaviors are ignored or if we rely on others to report them, the individual may execute an attack. It was a very tragic lesson learned in the aftermath of the Fort Hood shooting on November 5, 2009 where 13 personnel were killed and 29 others were wounded. In retrospect of this incident, had Major Hasan's leadership not ignored his obvious behavioral indicators and taken action against him, he probably wouldn't have carried out his planned and deliberate attack. It is everyone's responsibility to report radicalized personnel or HVEs; do not wait for someone else to report an obvious radical behavior. See something... Say Something!

THIS PAGE INTENTIONALLY LEFT BLANK

LIST OF REFERENCES

Air Safe Public Information. "Fatal Plane Crashes and Significant Events for the Boeing 727." Air Safe. http://www.airsafe.com/events/models/b727.htm. (accessed August 15, 2009),

Anonymous. "Theodore Kaczynski." *People Weekly,* December 30, 1996.

Associated Press. "Potential 'lone wolf' attackers concern police: Officials worry about disaffected men forming terrorism's next violent wave." MSNBC. http://www.msnbc.msn.com/id/8888865. (accessed May 20, 2009).

Barkun, Michael. *Religion and the Racist Right: The Origins of the Christian Identity Movement.* Chapel Hill, NC: University of North Carolina Press, 1997.

Barry, Ellen. "The Nation; Atlanta Olympics Bomber Apologizes to His Victims; Eric Rudolph, given four consecutive life terms, says he accepts responsibility." *The Los Angeles Times*, August 23, 2005.

————, and Jenny Jarvie. "The Nation: Rudolph Admits Bombing '96 Olympic Park; The defiant ex-fugitive cites hatred of abortion, government, sanctions." *Los Angeles Times*, April 14, 2005.

Begley, Sharon. "The Nature of Nurturing." *Newsweek*, March 27, 2000.

Burton, Fred, and Scott Stewart. "The Lone Wolf Disconnect." STRATFOR Global Intelligence, 2008. http://www.stratfor.com/weekly/lone_wolf_disconnect. (accessed October 20, 2009).

Chase, Alston. *A Mind for Murder: The Education of the Unabomber and the Origins of Modern Terrorism.* New York: W.W. Norton & Co., 2004.

Church, George. "The Matter of Tim McVeigh." *Time,* August 14, 1995.

Clutterbuck, Richard. *The Future of Political Violence: Destabilization, Disorder, and Terrorism.* New York: St. Martin's Press, 1986.

Combs, Cindy. *Terrorism in the Twenty-First Century: Fourth Edition.* Saddle River, NJ: Pearson Education, Inc., 2006.

Cooper, H.H.A. "What is a Terrorist: A Psychological Prospective." *Legal Medical Quarterly* (1977): 16. In *The Terrorist. Maxwell* Taylor. London: Brassey's Defence Publishers, 1998.

Crenshaw, Martha. *Encyclopedia of World Terrorism Volume II*. Armonk, New York: M.E. Sharpe Corp., 1997.

———. "Decisions to use Terrorism: Psychological Constraints on Instrumental Reasoning." In *Social Movements and Violence: Participation in Underground Organizations*, ed. Donatella della Porta. Greenwich, CT: JAI Press, Inc.

———. "The logic of Terrorism: Terrorist behavior as a product of strategic choice." In *Origins of Terrorism: Psychologies, Ideologies, Theologies, States of Mind.* By Walter Reich Washington D.C.: Woodrow Wilson Center Press, 1990.

Cuadros, Paul, Greg Fulton, Greg Land, Constance Richards. "How luck ran out for a most wanted fugitive" *TIME*, June 9, 2003.

Della Porta, Donatella. *Social Movements, Political Violence, and the State: A Comparative Analysis*. Cambridge, UK: Cambridge University Press, 1995.

Egan, Nancy. "Hunting Eric Rudolph." *Law Enforcement News* (2005): Vol 31, Issue 636, S5-S7.

Eggen, Dan. "Enthusiasts Eye Assault Rifles as Ban Nears End; Report: Makers Taking Orders." *The Washington Post,* September 8, 2004.

Ellul, Jacques. *The Technological Society.* New York: Vintage Books, 1967.

"Excerpts From the Unabomber's Journal." *The New York Times*, April 29, 1998.

Federal Bureau of Investigation. "Congressional Testimony 2002: "The threat of Eco-Terrorism." Federal Bureau of Investigation. http://www.fbi.gov/congress/congress02/jarboe021202.htm. (accessed May 20, 2009).

Fletcher, Michael. "At Home, Rudolph Wins Sympathy; Distrust of Government Widespread in Area." *The Washington Post,* June 4, 2003.

German, Mike. "Behind the Lone Terrorist, a Pack Mentality." *The Washington Post*, June 5, 2005.

Gitlin, Todd. "A Dangerous Mind." *The Washington Post,* March 2, 2003.

Hammer, David, and Jeffrey Paul, *Secrets Worth Dying For*. Bloomington, IN: 1st Books Library, 2004.

Jackson, David. "Man behind the mask." *Time,* November 17, 1997.

Johnston, David. "In Unabomber's Own Words, A Chilling Account of Murder." *The New York Times*, April 29, 1998.

Jonsson, Patrik. "How did Eric Rudolph Survive?." *The Christian Science Monitor*, June 4, 2003.

Judd, Alan. "Method in his Madness." *The Spectator,* September 6, 2003.

Juergensmeyer, Mark. *Terror in the Mind of God: The Global Rise of Religious Violence.* Berkeley, CA: University of California Press, 2003.

Kaczynski, Theodore. *The Unabomber Manifesto: Industrial Society & Its Future.* Minneapolis, MN: Filiquarian Publishing, LLC, 1998.

Kovaleski, Serge. "His Brother's Keeper." *The Washington Post*, July 10, 2001.

————. "His Brother's Keeper; When David Kaczynski let the FBI know that his older brother might be the Unabomber, he knew he was doing the right thing. But it's still hard to live with." *The Washington Post,* July 15, 2001.

Maslin, Janet. "The Unabomber and the 'Culture of Despair'." *New York Times,* March 3, 2003.

Mason, Carol. "The Hillbilly Defense: Culturally Mediating U.S. Terror at Home and Abroad." *NWSA Journal* (2005): Vol. 17, 3.

Michel, Lou, and Dan Herbeck. *American Terrorist.* New York: HarperCollins Publishers, 2001.

Moyano, Maria Jose. *Argentina's Lost Patrol.* New Haven, CT: Yale University Press, 1995.

Pearlstein, Richard. *The Mind of a Political Terrorist.* Wilmington, DE: Scholarly Resources Inc., 1991.

Rapoport, David, and Yonah Alexander. *The Rationalization of Terrorism.* Frederick, MD: University Publications of America, Inc., 1982.

Reeves, Jay. "Clinic Bomber Gets 2 Life Sentences; Rudolph is Unrepentant, Says Abortion Must Be Fought With Deadly Force." *The Washington Post*, July 19, 2005.

Romano, Lois. "An Enigma Awaits Death; Tim McVeigh Was a Good Kid and a Good Soldier. So What Went Wrong?." *The Washington Post,* May 4, 2001.

Russakoff, Dale, and Serge Kovaleski. "An Ordinary Boy's Extraordinary Rage; After a Long Search for Order, Timothy McVeigh Finally Found a World He Could Fit Into." *The Washington Post*, July 2, 1995.

Schuster, Henry, and Charles Stone. *Hunting Eric Rudolph: An Insider's Account of the Five-Year Search for the Olympic Bomber.* New York: Berkley Publishing Group, 2005.

Seegmiller, Beau. "Radicalized Margins: Eric Rudolph and Religious Violence." *Terrorism and Political* Violence. Volume 19, Number 4 (2007): 523.

Streitfeld, David. "Kaczynski, in Book, Says He's not Crazy." *The Washington Post,* February 12, 1999.

Stickney, Brandon. *All-American Monster: The Unauthorized Biography of Timothy McVeigh.* New York: Prometheus Books, 1996.

———. "Bombing suspect McVeigh a believer in strange government conspiracies." *The Skeptical Enquirer,* May/June 1997.

Taylor, Maxwell. *The Terrorist.* London: Brassey's Defence Publishers, 1988.

The Catholic Worker Movement. "Celebrating 75 Years 1933—2008." Catholic Worker. http://www.catholicworker.org/index.cfm. (accessed September 20, 2009).

Thomas, Jo. "McVeigh Described as Terrorist and as Victim of Circumstance." *New York Times,* May 30, 1997.

Turchie, Terry, and Kathleen Puckett. *Hunting the American Terrorist: The FBI's War on Homegrown Terror.* Palisades, NY: History Publishing Company, 2007.

Van Boven, Sara, and Patricia King. "A killer's self-portrait." *Newsweek,* May 11, 1998.

Vatz, Richard, and Lee Weinberg. "The Unabomber's twisted saga." *USA Today*, July 1998.

Verhovek, Sam. "Death in Waco: Scores die as compound is set on fire as FBI send tanks in with Tear gas." *The New York Times,* April 20, 1993.

Vollers, Maryanne. *Lone Wolf: Eric Rudolph and the Legacy of American Terror.* New York: Harper Perennial Publishing Company, 2007.

———. *Lone Wolf: Eric Rudolph: Murder, Myth, and the Pursuit of an American Outlaw.* New York: HarperCollins, 2006.

Waits, Chris, and David Shors. *Unabomber: The Secret Life of Ted* Kaczynski. Helena, MT: Helena Independent Record and Montana Magazine, 1999.

Walls, Kathleen. *Man Hunt: The Eric Rudolph Story.* LaVergne, TN: Global Authors Publications, 2003.

Witkin, Gordan. "The nightmare of Idaho's Ruby Ridge." *U.S. News and World Report,* September 11, 1995.

Home-Grown Violent Extremist and Recognizing Indicators of Radicalization

While prosecuting the war on terrorism abroad, along with the implementation of enhanced security measures, we've been fairly successful in deterring attacks in the United States. To counter our efforts, Al-Qaeda and other terrorist organizations have adapted their tactics for recruiting and radicalizing individuals in order to carry out attacks on us and our allies. While it's still possible to recruit individuals, organize them into cells, and conduct organized attacks using their usual methodology, centrally controlled or dictated attacks are the exception and not the rule. In our country, the attacks are less sophisticated and carried out by radicalized individuals typically described as "lone wolves" or as we say in Army-speak, "Homegrown Violent Extremists (HVE). From 2001 to 2009, there were 91 HVE attacks against the US. The recruitment of lone wolf terrorists is especially insidious since recruited individuals don't fit the typical "terrorist mold" with most being U.S. citizens without any criminal record, without long-term exposure to radical Islamic influences, having adequate or above-average educations, and working decent jobs.

While we can statistically categorize people who are typically susceptible or at high risk for terrorist recruitment and radicalization, surveilling this segment of the population would not be legal or practical; therefore, we must understand the process of the recruitment and radicalization of lone wolf terrorists and recognize the indicators of radicalization so that we can foil their plots and incarcerate them.

Most experts describe the Radicalization Process in four distinct stages:

☐ Stage 1: Pre-Radicalization
☐ Stage 2: Self-Identification
☐ Stage 3: Indoctrination
☐ Stage 4: Jihadization

In the first stage, Pre-Radicalization, individuals typically lead "ordinary" lives. As stated before, they come from nearly all walks of life (professional, blue-collar, white-collar, military, etc.), typically having no criminal history and working ordinary jobs. Then, something tragic occurs in their rather "uneventful lives" where these individuals are alienated or disassociated from the rest of society. This event could be losing a job, losing an investment, a divorce, a tragic accident, or a death in the family. Sometimes, these types of events affect our soldiers also placing them at risk for recruitment. When this occurs, these individuals search for spiritual guidance and give them cause to seek meaning to their existence, or, perhaps, find group membership to fill gaps left by a broken or failing family (Stage 2, Self-Identification). While there are a number of paths for these individuals to realize their new identity (such as schools, mosques where radical Imams preach, or in prisons), most often, they turn to the most convenient, non-intimidating path providing a sense of anonymity and security, the Internet. Self-radicalization begins the day that an individual seeks out jihadist websites. Continued online association or correspondence may point him/her to other resources like other local jihadist mentors and likeminded fanatics furthering his/her Indoctrination (Stage 3). When the individual has been sufficiently indoctrinated and convinced to take action to support the cause of Radical Islamic Jihad, he/she has entered the final and most dangerous stage of the Radicalization Process. It is at this stage, when we depend on our ability to recognize the Indicator of Radicalization.

Over the years, experts have determined behavior patterns common to HVEs. These behavior patterns are the following:

1. Advocating violence, the threat of violence, or use of force to achieve goals that are political, religious, or ideological in nature.

2. Advocating support for international terrorist organizations or objectives.

3. Providing financial or other material support to a terrorist organization or to someone suspected of being a terrorist.

4. Association with or connections to known or suspected terrorists.

5. Repeated expression of hatred and intolerance of American society, culture, government, or principles of the U.S. Constitution.

6. Repeated visiting or browsing of Internet websites that promote of advocate violence directed against the United States of U.S. forces, or that promote International Terrorism or terrorist themes without official sanction in the performance of duties.

7. Expressing an obligation to engage in violence in support of International Terrorism or inciting others to do the same.

8. Purchasing bomb making materials or obtaining information about the construction of explosives.

9. Active attempts to encourage others to violate laws, disobey lawful orders or regulations, or disrupt military activities.

10. Family ties to known or suspected international terrorist or terrorist supporters.

Although there are many of us who might have reservations on reporting individuals exhibiting these behaviors because we might be labeled as racists, bigots, or not supporting Army Equal Employment Opportunity (EEO), it must be understood, that if these behaviors are ignored or if we rely on others to report them, the individual may execute an attack. It was a very tragic lesson learned in the aftermath of the Fort Hood shooting on November 5, 2009 where 13 personnel were killed and 29 others were wounded. In retrospect of this incident, had Major Hasan's leadership not ignored his obvious behavioral indicators and taken action against him, he probably wouldn't have carried out his planned and deliberate attack. It is everyone's responsibility to report radicalized personnel or HVEs; do not wait for someone else to report an obvious radical behavior. See something… Say Something!

www.ingramcontent.com/pod-product-compliance
Lightning Source LLC
Chambersburg PA
CBHW081118290526

45795CB00006B/2167